TOWARD AWAKENING

Jean Vaysse was born in Le Mans in France in 1917. Following his father and grandfather into the medical profession, he became one of the best surgeons in Paris, well known for his care and ingenuity, a pioneer in the development of open heart surgery and transplantations. He was a student of Gurdjieff's for many years, working in the Gurdjieff groups in Paris and later helping to lead them through the 1960s. He died in 1975.

JEAN VAYSSE

TOWARD AWAKENING

AN APPROACH TO THE TEACHING LEFT BY GURDJIEFF

LONDON AND NEW YORK

First published in 1980
ARKANA edition 1988
ARKANA PAPERBACKS is an imprint of
Routledge
11 New Fetter Lane, London EC4P 4EE

Published in the USA by
ARKANA (Routledge, Chapman and Hall, Inc.)
29 West 35th Street, New York, NY 10001

Printed in Great Britain
by Guernsey Press Co. Ltd.,
Guernsey, Channel Islands

Library of Congress Cataloguing in Publication Data
Vaysse, Jean.
Toward awakening.

Translation of: Vers l'éveil à sopi-même.
1.Gurdjieff, Georges Ivanovitch, 1872–1949.
I. Title.
B4249.G84V3913 1988 197'.2 87–33690
ISBN 1–85063–115–8 (pbk.)

Library of Congress CIP Data also available
ISBN 1–85063–115–8

Foreword

IN his introduction to *Meetings with Remarkable Men*, Gurdjieff puts into the mouth of an elderly, intelligent Persian a long tirade against all forms of modern Western literature, which he says contain nothing substantial for the perfecting of humanity. "It is all exterior," the Persian says . . . "An Asiatic, having lost to a lesser degree the ability to feel, that is to say, standing closer to nature, half-consciously feels and instinctively senses the [Western] writer's complete lack of any knowledge of reality and of any genuine understanding of the subject he is writing about."

One of Gurdjieff's greatest pupils, P. D. Ouspensky, a writer by profession, remarked similarly that "many people find it easier to talk, and particularly to write about things they don't know. It is much more difficult to write about things one does know."

Obviously, these considerations may be applied, and even apply specially, to books about Gurdjieff's teaching itself. Indeed, at the risk of appearing to make a secret of the ideas, the small groups studying with Gurdjieff, Ouspensky and others between the wars made a rather strict principle of not talking publicly or publishing anything about their activities, even though careful notes were kept. It was not made easy for new people to find the groups and, once they had been accepted, ideas and readings from Gurdjieff's and Ouspensky's unpublished manuscripts were given only occasionally and not always in logical succession.

When *Beelzebub's Tales* and Ouspensky's *In Search of the Miraculous* were published by Gurdjieff around the time of his death in 1949, the situation changed. First one pupil, then another, evidently without much mutual consultation, has written down and published their version of the teaching until now, besides all Gurdjieff's own writings, at least one hundred other books about him and his teaching are available in the English language alone. Given the Persian's warning that nothing is harder than to write something that is of substantial help, these books—even if they are not all of the same quality—are a remarkable testimony to the courage and energy of mind generated in the Work.

Parallel with the appearance of these books, groups studying Gurdjieff's method orally have sprung up all over the world. Almost without exception, they continue to meet privately and to avoid most forms of promotion and publicity. This is not to protect or suppress secret knowledge left by Gurdjieff but on account of his insistence that real understanding of the teaching takes so much time and effort that the ideas are certain to be distorted if they are written down and shared too soon and indiscriminately. At the same time, with the spreading impact of Gurdjieff's message, which corresponds so exactly to the needs of modern people for something between Western and Eastern thought, between modern science and ancient knowledge—that partakes of the energy in both but is neither—it is certain that still more books will be written.

In these circumstances, obviously each student who was close to Gurdjieff or his principal pupils will sooner or later have to face the question of whether to write down and publish what he remembers and what he is tiying to transmit. In deciding whether or not to write and to publish, each—according to the level at which he understands the task of reaping the harvest of what Gurdjieff sowed—will have to take into account the situation of the teaching as it now exists everywhere and the entire body of writings that is already available.

Jean Vaysse was born at Le Mans in France in 1917. Following his father and grandfather in the medical profession, he became one of the best surgeons in Paris, well-known for his care and ingenuity, a pioneer in the development of open heart surgery and transplantations. He was a polished speaker and lecturer. With dark, searching eyes and a somewhat hard, pitiless face, even a brief acquaintanceship with him left an impression of great intensity. His patients trusted him. He was deeply sensible of their anxiety and spent hours discussing their health and talking with them about Far Eastern art and his collection of antiques. In his spare time he was an abstract painter, as well as a student of metaphysics.

As he himself says about Gurdjieff's ideas, which he met through a student friend before any of the books were published, "whoever approaches them for the first time without prejudice feels touched to the core by a truth which he cannot deny and called upon to put in question all the values his life has been based on until then."

Working in the groups in Paris and later helping to lead them through the 1960's, Jean Vaysse felt the time had come to express Gurdjieff's written teaching in a more coherent and logical way in order to bring it within the reach of the average educated reader. He was impressed with the conciseness and exactness achieved by Ouspensky in his lectures published as *The Psychology of Man's Possible Evolution* and, although not a writer, wished to see if a more detailed, expanded introduction to the ideas could be produced.

The book that resulted, *Vers l'eveil a soi-meme*, after going through some revisions, was published in France not long before Jean Vaysse's untimely death in 1975. This translation is offered to English-speaking readers with the permission of Madame Annie Vaysse and the family.

Vaysse's book is based on Gurdjieff's own books and Ouspensky's *In Search of the Miraculous* but it must not be dismissed as a mere paraphrase of Ouspensky. *In Search* was written and meticulously revised by Ouspensky over a period of at least ten years in order to give as honest and objective an account of the teaching as possible. Probably his achievement will never be equaled. In any case it was intended to preserve the teaching in as pure and impersonal a form as possible.

Jean Vaysse softens the rather terrifying impact of Gurdjieff's teaching as it is transmitted by Ouspensky. He gives substance to the ideas, several of which have become popular in modern psychology, and—without detracting too much from what the pupil has to do for himself—begins to show how they are related together. His book is one of the first accounts to hint at the practical approach to work through giving attention to the sensation of the body, a study of which was central in Gurdjieff's method and which has been carefully transmitted by Madame Jeanne de Salzmann.

There is no vision without true ideas and, as Ouspensky demonstrated in *In Search of the Miraculous*, Gurdjieff brought great ideas to life with no mean hand. As has been said, the first impact of his ideas is to put into question everything on which men base their lives, to help us become still. That is the first unforgettable impact, but it needs to be repeated as many times as we forget! Gradually it becomes clear that these eternally existing ideas, as we learn them in books and diagrams, are not given as a blueprint of principles to be defended or aimed for, but as a sort of starter or catalyst for the all-round moral effort that is the price of all real knowledge. "Once the head has remembered," Gurdjieff said, "let it go."

But we are going too fast. Learning the new language, as Jean Vaysse says, is the first payment that has to be made in approaching our work toward awakening. Vaysse adds the word "presence" to the new words that are needed. For the uninitiated beginner, to be present means trying to remember an idea with the head or, if the idea is taken with feeling, it amounts to a task of frightening proportions. But these attempts to enforce the idea of being present are distinct from and even contradictory to the sensation, once one "lets the head free," that I am here now in this immediate space in contact with a life-force which supports, enlightens and unifies my presence.

The very beginning of Work is in learning and gradually opening to the place of presence and its relative levels—for example, in the relationship between older and younger people or between the questions that people ask and how they are answered. From this point of view, the knowledge we are searching for is much more than what can be written in books or told in words. It is an immersion in experience. Gurdjieff rediscovered a method to initiate the experiencing of self-knowledge and knowledge of life; this experiencing is what Vaysse wished to enable more people to approach by means of his book.

JOHN PENTLAND

Faith of consciousness is freedom
Faith of feeling is weakness
Faith of body is stupidity.

Love of consciousness evokes the same in response
Love of feeling evokes the opposite
Love of body depends on type and polarity.

Hope of consciousness is strength
Hope of feeling is slavery
Hope of body is disease.

G. I. Gurdjieff
Beelzebub's Tales to His Grandson, p. 361

CONTENTS

TOWARD AWAKENING

The ideas we shall deal with here represent only one aspect of the teaching transmitted during his life by G. I. [illegible] They assume their real sense only as one [illegible]

[illegible]

[illegible] (London: Routledge & Kegan Paul [illegible]

[illegible]

Introduction

THE ideas we shall deal with here represent only one aspect of the teaching transmitted during his life by G. I. Gurdjieff. They acquire their real sense only as one of the elements of a greater whole upon which—for every man who recognizes its necessity—the work of inner transformation is based.

These ideas were expounded, first and foremost, by Gurdjieff himself in his writings[1]—in the form of hints, to be sure, yet with masterly breadth of vision. They have been echoed with remarkable fidelity in *In Search of the Miraculous* by P. D. Ouspensky.[2]

Actually, their meaning and real importance first became apparent in the living experience which Gurdjieff provided for his students, not only by his explanations and by his direct answers to their questions, or by exercises corresponding to the stages of their development, but also, and above all, by having them participate in the tests offered by life itself.

It was Jeanne de Salzmann's achievement to preserve and transmit in all their original authenticity not only the written part, but also the oral and practical parts, of the teaching given by Gurdjieff, which without her would surely have been lost. We owe her everything that has reached us.

1. G. I. Gurdjieff, *All and Everything* (London: Routledge & Kegan Paul, 1950, 1963).

2. P. D. Ouspensky, *In Search of the Miraculous* (London: Routledge & Kegan Paul, 1950). See also P. D. Ouspensky's *The Psychology of Man's Possible Evolution* (London: Routledge & Kegan Paul, 1951). Although they deal with little more than the first stages of this teaching, reading both these books of Ouspensky is invaluable for anyone who wishes to go deeply into these ideas. Gurdjieff's own book provides a more complete view of the ideas, but is more difficult to approach.

Brought to the Western World in this particular period, Gurdjieff's ideas contain what is probably the truest answer to the questions raised by the tremendous material power now in the hands of modern man as he questions himself in front of the so-called "options" which its use obliges him to face.

These ideas, fundamentally in accord with the traditional teachings of the Great Knowledge, make strikingly clear the deep chasm that has opened up between what they represent and our contemporary way of living and thinking. Whoever meets them without prejudice for the first time feels touched to the heart by a force of truth that cannot be denied, and also called on to put into question all the values which until then have supported him through life.

To make this first contact is often difficult, and it is here that the author wishes to make a contribution by helping to get them better known.

Being the work of one man, this attempt to restate in an accessible form the main points of this new "doctrine of awakening" is of necessity limited. The following chapters are the written record of a series of preliminary explanations addressed to people of different backgrounds who had shown a desire to undertake a study of this teaching. That is why a considerable amount of material borrowed from the previously mentioned works will be found here.

Some redundancy has been allowed in order that each of the following essays should constitute a whole in itself, and for this the author asks to be excused. Since words have a relative meaning, the question of language had to be taken into account. For, while the vocabulary employed by Gurdjieff is very simple, the meaning of some of the words he used is not always the same as that finally imposed on them in other contemporary systems of ideas. Moreover, the meaning of certain words depends on the reader's level of understanding, and their "real" meaning may be very different from their everyday usage. Words which lend themselves to confusion in one way or another are placed in quotation marks.

We realize that the general form of this book does not make for easy reading, but for various reasons this form seems to us valid. While one may not understand at all how such ideas can appear and develop, it is obvious that a condensation of this kind is the result of a long collective work in front of which personality can only stand aside and make way for the deeper meaning of the thought. By finding again and again in himself the taste of this attitude, may the reader of these pages receive practical help in his own search for an unchangeable truth!

Questions

I

In the universe we live in, it is obvious that nothing is lost. Everything comes from somewhere and, having been changed or transformed to some degree, returns somewhere. Nothing which has taken form or is alive remains immutable, and each of these changes serves life in some fashion. A human being cannot be an exception to this universal principle. Being endowed with thought, how can a man go through life without questioning himself? and, being endowed with feeling, how can he remain indifferent to such questioning?

II

Mineral, vegetable, animal, human, each kingdom or genus of life on our planet is the bearer of a specific quality which characterizes it and which, within a certain range of variation, it has the mission to develop. Being endowed with thought, is a man not bound to ask himself what is the specific characteristic of human life, which human life alone can develop? One day, should he arrive at an answer which seems valid, can a man worthy of the name have any other aim than to try to nourish from then on, by all available means, this quality proper to him and his brothers?

III

Once a man has realized that he ought to get to the root of things, and that he can no longer be content with living in accordance with the demands of the ordinary world, then a question arises about what he himself is and about the meaning of his own life. In the beginning, the way he searches and the way he puts this question to himself can take very different forms. But finally, beyond the partial aspects, which appear at first to be the only ones, does not all search in this field come to be seen as one—that of knowing, behind appearances, what is true? And, in the end, is not every man who asks himself this question, definitely and essentially a seeker of the truth?

Inner life and outer life: an overview

MANY indications, which impartial observation can soon transform into conviction, lead us to feel that there are two natures in us. One of them is personal or individual, is relatively accessible to our usual means of perception, and is both organic and psychic (or animal and animated). The other, much less easy to perceive, is experienced as our participation in something far greater than the individual. Thus we call it spiritual, even universal; and, in fact, we hardly know how to speak about it. The attention paid to it varies a great deal from person to person and at different moments of life: almost everybody, however, will recognize that, at least at certain moments, he has felt, alongside an egocentric, selfish tendency, this need for something infinite or "absolute."

From the moment a man turns toward himself like this, questions himself, and struggles to understand both what he is and what he could be, it becomes clear that he can turn in either of two ways and have two kinds of so-called "activities," two kinds of life going in different directions. One is entirely oriented toward the outside, and is centered chiefly on the efficiency, usefulness and productivity of "the individual" within the framework of his society. This is the way of living that western civilization has developed: in order to succeed each member pursues years of education, character development, apprenticeship, study, specialization, "recycling," etc., and the resulting effectiveness in outer life is the main value by which he is classified. The other way to turn, the other kind of "activity," concerns the inner life: it is centered above all on the "realization" of the latent possibilities contained within the individual. It develops the faculties and qualities characteristic of his human nature, and hence the accession to (or return from) levels of life or worlds of which outer life has no suspicion. This way of living, while very little known in western civilization, is what has been specially developed in certain strata of Oriental civilizations. For those who take it up, its development demands even more time and care, more learning, research and methodical studies, than are required by outer life.

These two kinds of life can seem contradictory at first, and, indeed, in a certain way, they are. It is obvious, however, that each corresponds to one of our natures, and that a complete man must live both at the same time: they are his human nature, which thus includes within itself a permanent contradiction.

Those great teachings and traditional ways which have remained complete and have not forgotten either of the two aspects of man tell us, each in its own way, that these two natures show that man belongs to two great currents of equal importance, which flow through the existing universe and assure its equilibrium. One is the current of creation which, originating from the highest level, flows into diverse forms of manifestation and, in this sense, is an involutionary movement. The other is the current that may be called "spiritualizing"; for, issuing from manifested forms, it returns to the source (to "God") and is thus an evolutionary current. By virtue of his dual nature and the two facets of his life, man belongs to both currents (he has "his feet on earth and his head in the heavens"), and he is one of the bridges, one of the levels at which exchange takes place, a "mediator" between the two. Could it be that this "mediating"—which can prevent him from being lost in one current or the other—is a measure of his growth while at the same time it gives him his third aspect?

What matters to us chiefly at this point, placed as we are solely, or almost solely, in the outer life, is that we know, or think we know, one of these two natures: that by which we live daily, our ordinary nature. Life calls to it incessantly and it always responds. The other nature is hidden behind it, more and more forgotten: at first, its life is displaced and slowed down; later, it is submerged and drowned in the unconscious, and finally lost. So far as it is not too deeply buried, this other nature springs up unexpectedly now and then in moments of lucidity. Suddenly we are forced (usually at difficult times) to recognize it without knowing where it comes from. Compared with what we ordinarily are, these moments have such a special flavor for us that they do not leave us altogether in peace; we retain an aftertaste of our inadequacy and an uneasy conscience, aware that we are not what we ought to be. But we have no need at all of such moments in order to live, and, if we want to feel comfortable again, we have only to forget them—which we are all the more prone to do because everything around us is so arranged as to encourage this forgetting. However, if a man wants to be fully himself one day, the re-establishment of the lost balance between his two natures and his two ways of living is certainly the first work which is necessary. This is why all that follows is addressed only to those who are attentive to these special moments, and, wishing to be clearer about what they stand for, accept the ensuing discomfort in their lives. Inner evolution and the work that it requires cannot be carried out effectively unless set in motion by a genuine awareness of our inadequacies and faults (Gurdjieff used to say, our nothingness). Along with this comes the discomfort inherent in the resurgence within us of our second nature which was neglected or forgotten in our upbringing, and for the inner contradictions and conflicts which this resurgence engenders. Nothing is ever given free—to accept this inevitable discomfort is the first payment man must make when he sets out in search of himself.

In this search there is perhaps a risk of oscillating between an imbecilic bliss (which would be deliberately ignoring the discomfort) and a kind of masochism (giving it undue importance—has it not been called by some, metaphysical anguish?). The only right attitude, a difficult one to be sure, is somewhere between the two—the recognition of the precise nature of our uneasiness and our inner conflict, such as they are, in the hope of resolving them.

Obviously such a hope and such an undertaking are conceivable only if we have the data in front of us. This is why the question of what we are in reality, in each of our two natures, as in all that depends on them, appears from the first as the most fundamental question of all. For a man who wishes to be wholly himself one day, the search for the truth of what he is is the most urgent necessity. It is this search which leads to that knowledge of oneself with which all traditional schools are concerned.

That knowledge, furthermore, cannot be limited to knowledge of oneself. How can individuality assume its full meaning unless it is re-situated in its general context? Man participates in the totality of life on earth: he is one of its elements, perhaps the principal one, and the study of its meaning is inseparable from the study of himself. Moreover, the life on earth in which man participates is itself only one step, at one level, which has its place and its role in the exchange of forces within the solar system to which the earth belongs. This solar system again is only one among many others; and, finally, in order to be complete, the study of man, the study of oneself, has to be placed within a general cosmic perspective.

Man is such a complex being that he can be studied in very different ways, which take into account more or less adequately his structure and the relationships between his different parts. The most complete and the most useful view for the search we are undertaking considers that his organic body, the only one immediately and directly accessible, is made up of a number of different organic and "psychological" functions, and that these are directed by centers which give to the basic vital energy the specific form proper to each function. The organic body consists of a combination of individual qualities. Some of these are inborn and together constitute the basic initial aspect of each man. They can therefore be called his essence. The rest are a collection of acquired characteristics superimposed by the environment during the course of life. Because of this added-on character (put on like a theatrical mask—*persona*), they can be called his personality. Actually, this so-called personality, the form in which a man's various elements are grouped together, is constructed in each man around as few as two or three or even around only one fundamental feature of his essence, thus giving a particular flavor to everything that is crystallized in his person. Also, each man's personality is structured in a different way, more or less stereotyped by the different situations with which the environment habitually confronts him. Thus, in the course of his life, one man acquires many personal qualities, many personages, many "I's" (because each, speaking for itself independently of the others, says "I," "me," when it appears).

In addition to this organic life, a man participates in other levels of life which are less immediately accessible: a psychic (or rather animate) life, no doubt also a spiritual life, and perhaps still others, each having its own basis, faculties and function in him. Man also passes through various states—sleep, dreaming, waking, and sometimes moments of a much greater "opening" to life—moments of awakening to beauty, to harmony and to a need for the infinite, which are in fact, without his knowing it, moments of awakening to his inner being. A man sees these various states coming and going in himself in a more or less haphazard way and often they escape him altogether. In the midst of all this, certain things develop in us. We make up our own ideas and fantasies about ourselves and the world we live in. We have a sensitivity, desires and emotions which color our lives in a style peculiar to us. We have our own particular ways of behaving in our outer as in our inner life. But without doubt, the most fundamental characteristic, although at the same time the least apparent—it has to be looked for in order to find it—is the incredible mechanicalness of the whole thing. Through a combination of habits, automatic reactions and conditionings established by repetition in the course of life, it is all self-sustaining and very soon encloses itself within limits from which it no longer emerges.

Nevertheless, we have in ourselves at certain moments an intuition that something else is possible—an indestructible inner freedom, a harmonious unity, and participation in the life of a "better" world. Certain myths, certain forms of art, the traditions and religions are influences which seem to come from "somewhere else," touch us sometimes in the midst of our ordinary life and revive this intuition. Indeed, these influences bring us an impression of inner opening, an opportunity to awaken, and if we are attentive to it, we can recognize that something in ourselves responds—a religious feeling or an inner "spiritual" sense, which we feel uplifts us. In this way, there can be developed in certain people a special, almost magnetic sensitivity and attraction to everything that can lead in this direction. More and more clearly the question arises: would it not be possible to give my life a quality other than that which I ordinarily see in it—that very quality that I glimpse only in moments of "awakening"?

Writings and books tell us about this. They speak of an inner life possible for man, and of a transformation culminating in a "realization" which is called by different names according to the different paths. They speak of higher bodies with a life, faculties and development of their own; they speak of the self—real or unreal—of its evolution, of going beyond it. Everything could be found in books if we were able to understand them.

But all this accumulated information, these experiences and the conclusions drawn from them, belong to other people. For us, all this is theoretical. We may perhaps believe it insofar as it does not conflict with our experience or with ideas we have already acquired; but, in fact, the conclusions of others can really convince us only to the extent that we discover them again for ourselves. Books can help guide our experience, but we can never be sure except of that which we have verified and lived through ourselves. To this question of a possible evolution, the only answer we can believe reaches us through experience personally lived through. In the beginning, no doubt, we have nothing much to impel us toward such an endeavor; outer life absorbs us completely, and everything this experience requires has to be found at the expense of outer life. However, if we wish to know, the only way is to try with what we have. Where can we start from? Simply from a deep self-questioning, from the need for an answer, from the intuition that this answer does actually exist, and from evidence that if we want to go toward it we must draw from our everyday life the energies and time needed for such a search. It is an immense task of which we know nothing and in front of which we see clearly that, if we start out alone on the adventure, we will more than likely get lost, become exhausted or fail. But, as in all large human enterprises, we can perhaps find other men likewise prepared to work toward a clear knowledge of what they are. Alone or with others, we may hope in turning toward another level of life that the forces active on that level have need of us also, and will send us the help we need.

Undoubtedly, such were the *raisons d'etre* for schools and ways. Among them, one can distinguish various kinds, according to whether they are connected with the way of imitation, the way of revelation, or the way of understanding, and each of these ways is based mostly, indeed exclusively, on certain specific human possibilities. There are thus three principal categories: the way to mastery of the body (that of the fakir), the way to mastery of the emotions (that of the monk), and the way to intellectual mastery (that of the yogi). All these ways demand that a man withdraw at the outset from ordinary life and devote himself to the life he has chosen. But in the present state of the world is it possible to cut oneself off in this way from daily life? Does the present age still allow a man to develop only one aspect of himself and to give up the possibility of a harmonious and complete development which is inherent in the whole man?

Or, even knowing that, on the whole, the work, effort and sacrifices will be as great as, and perhaps greater than, in the other ways, is not a real work on oneself and a complete development for man possible, at the present time, in life itself? Was this not always possible according to hidden ways? And for the world we live in, has it not become an imperative necessity? This is the question which is now in front of us and to which no theoretical answer will ever be a satisfactory response.

The meaning of self-study

As soon as we begin to question ourselves about our own identity and nature, either as a result of shocks in life or under the influence of exceptional moments, the question arises as to whether, instead of giving ourselves up more or less completely to events and thus to a course of evolution which we cannot control at all, there might not be in that evolution something which depends on us and could be influenced by us.

Thus it becomes obvious that the wish to be fully himself will not leave a man completely unaffected, and his first necessity, which is as urgent as the organic need to eat, should be to find out if something in this direction is effectively possible for him, and in what way.

We can look outside us for the answer in books, philosophical systems and doctrines, in what the religions say—and, for a while, these answers may satisfy us. They satisfy us so long as life has not seriously brought us to question their effectiveness. Put to the test in life, the most solid religious faith in revealed truth is finally shaken, if it is not supported and confirmed in lived experiences. And, furthermore, we are so made that we rely indelibly and unshakably on what we have lived and verified for ourselves, in ourselves, by ourselves.

If we question ourselves deeply about ourselves and our possible evolution, we see it is within ourselves and through ourselves that we shall ultimately have to find the answer. And if we ponder what is the meaning of this world around us, it is again only in ourselves and through ourselves that an answer can come that we recognize to be our own, and in which we can have faith. In addition, self-knowledge has from the beginning of time been fundamental in many doctrines and many schools. Not an exterior analytical knowledge, such as modern western science has been pursuing for so long, avoiding all the inner questions or trying to reduce them to purely materialistic explanations, but rather an inner self-knowledge wherein, to avoid distortion, each element, each structure, each function, as well as their relationships and the laws which govern them, are not looked at only from the outside, but must be experienced in the whole context to which they belong and can only be truly known "at work" in that totality. This is a completely different attitude from that which modern science has accustomed us to, and the one does not exclude the other. But, for our possibility of inner evolution, one thing must be clear. What is required is not intellectual knowledge, which, properly speaking, is mere information. Such information may be necessary, but is absolutely inadequate in our search. For this search, the self-knowledge we need is above all an inner experience, consciously lived, of what we are, including the whole range of impressions of oneself which one receives.

A man cannot attain knowledge of this order except at the price of long work and patient efforts. Self-knowledge is inseparable from the Great Knowledge, objective Knowledge. It goes by stages, the first of which may appear simple to start with; however, even for one who recognizes the need of it, it soon comes to seem an immense undertaking with an almost unreachable goal. Little by little an unsuspected complexity is revealed.

It gradually becomes clear that the study of man has no meaning unless it is placed in the context of life as a whole and of the whole world in which he lives. The study of man is inseparable from a living study of the cosmos. Thus, obstacles never cease to arise, and this search, which at first may appear straightforward, opens up finally onto horizons of which a man could hardly have had the slightest idea when he began.

To have any chance of reaching his aim without going astray or getting lost, a man needs a guide for the study of himself. Here as elsewhere, he must learn from those who know, and accept to be guided by those who have already trodden the same path. Real self-knowledge requires a school. It cannot be found in books, which can give only theoretical data, mere information, leaving the whole of the real work still to be done —transforming the information into understanding, and then the understanding into self-knowledge.

In the beginning, the only thing that can be asked of a man who engages in this search is that he should understand the necessity of making his way tirelessly along the path whatever happens, and that he should understand that nothing but self-study, rightly conducted, can lead him to self-knowledge and the Great Knowledge.

Right observation of oneself

THE first step in a study intended to lead to self-knowledge is self-observation. However, this has to be practiced in a way that corresponds to the aim. Thus, the ordinary kind of self-observation which people practice all their lives is almost entirely useless, and, in fact, brings nothing valid for the self-knowledge we need, a knowledge experienced and lived through.

There are actually two methods of self-observation: analysis and a simple recording of impressions.

Self-analysis or introspection is the usual method applied in modern psychology, though at the present time there is a movement away from it. In this method each observed fact is taken by itself and serves as the basis for intellectual analysis, in the form of questions about its causes, connections and implications. What caused this, why did it happen? Why did it happen this way and not some other way? The observed fact is taken as the center of gravity of the inquiry, and the other factors are grouped in relation to it and not in relation to the whole man. The man as a whole, although not completely disregarded, is relegated to second place. But the analysis of an isolated phenomenon, taken apart from its context and apart from general laws, makes absolutely no sense and is simply a waste of time.

Furthermore, a man who observes himself in this way begins to look for answers to what he sees, then becomes interested in the answers and their consequences and soon loses sight of his original intention which was to observe himself, not to make interpretations for which he does not yet have the necessary material. Thus an entire intellectual process develops around the observation, which becomes of secondary importance and is even forgotten. A man who analyzes himself like this not only makes no progress toward self-knowledge, but even inflates ideas or fantasies about himself which in some cases become the worst obstacles to attaining this knowledge; and so he goes away from what he was searching for.

Another very bad effect of this analytical method is that it makes for arbitrary divisions of the functions of the man who studies himself in this way; whichever function is predominant (almost always the intellectual) stands apart from all the other functions and looks at them in its own way, and often evaluates or judges all of them as though it understood them. Such an attitude can but increase the predominance of one function over the others and does nothing to redress the balance between them. The inner dissociation and conflict inherent in everyone is thus immediately reinforced.

The analytic method may be useful very much later, perhaps to deepen the knowledge of a particular point when a sufficient sense of the whole to which it belongs has been acquired, and this without losing sight of that whole. But to arrive at self-knowledge and allow a harmonious evolution to take place, self-observation should not, to begin with, under any pretext be an analysis or an attempt to analyze.

In the beginning, only the method of recording impressions can lead to the aim we have in view. No observation has any real value for self-knowledge unless it is looked at in relation to the whole structure of the observer, and unless connected with all those elements and laws by which this structure is formed, not only as it is now, but as it is intended to become—that is, in the movement and the life of the whole. While these "constatations" are going on, the whole must never be lost sight of for a moment; it is all that counts and it must remain the center of gravity.

For this reason, all results or former experiences of self-observation must be laid aside. It is not that they have to be systematically rejected, for we cannot live without them—and, incidentally, there may be very valuable elements in them. But all this material has been brought together by ideas about oneself, and about various divisions of oneself, which are incomplete or erroneous, so that in its present form it is of no use for the work we are undertaking; whatever may be valid in this material will become available again at the proper time and will be put in its proper place.

Right self-observation directed toward self-knowledge is possible only if precise conditions are first prepared.

So that it can begin without being destructive, certain pieces of information have first to be provided as a sort of baggage—inevitably intellectual at this stage. The first work for anyone who really wishes to observe himself is to verify this information in his own experience as soon as he can, and not to accept anything as true which he has not authenticated in this way by himself.

The necessary pieces of information concern the structure itself of the human being, his way of functioning, and his most immediate possible transformations. They must be presented in a form complete enough to serve as the framework and scaffolding for what will later become real self-knowledge.

While this work of verifying the information is going on, self-study has to begin at the beginning—that is, one starts to observe oneself by simply recording impressions without judging or changing anything, as if one did not know oneself at all and had never observed oneself before, trying only to see to which center or group of centers the observed phenomena belong, with which functions they are connected, and with what level of those functions.

As soon as the first steps are taken, one finds that there are considerable obstacles and that there is no hope of eventually overcoming them if they are not first seen just as they are.

It is also obvious that energy, time and special conditions are indispensable for such work. How shall we find the energy unless we first look to see what forces we can count on in ourselves and around ourselves, and then consider how to find the time and the necessary conditions?

There is practically no chance for one man alone to resolve so many and such various difficulties, no matter how good his original intentions.

He very quickly needs two kinds of help. On the one hand, he needs the inner help that self-observation itself can bring. Besides what it enables him to see about the way we are made, it soon shows him that one part of the whole is functioning wrongly and is taking up all the room for itself. This view of the situation, for a man who is seeking to be fully himself, arouses a wish for certain changes and for transformation. This vision and the wish it awakens are the prime force on which all further work depends. But this inner help, this ally in himself, cannot be enough. Contrary to what he usually believes, one man alone cannot know what needs to be changed nor how to change it. He needs, as soon as possible, help from the outside, and to find a school where the conditions—of which he himself knows nothing—actually exist for allowing this transformation he wishes for to pursue its course.

For a man who has become aware of his situation, finding a school becomes the most urgent necessity.

A simple overall view of the structure of man

BEFORE real self-observation can begin, and with it the recording of valid impressions, a first step is necessary. In fact, valid self-observation is not possible unless certain data have previously been provided about what we are and about the possibilities inherent in human life. These data can become of real value for us only if afterward we can verify them, step by step, by ourselves; and thus arrive both at a clear enough view of the whole and sufficient practical experience to correctly situate subsequent observations in a soundly based framework, without rejecting out of hand the various suggestions that life offers us, but also without letting ourselves be naively swallowed up or uselessly distracted by them. Afterward, we shall have to bring all these data into question again, item by item; but since time is short for the journey ahead, there is a need that overall views should be opened up for us at the beginning and remain available to help us through the entire period of our search.

These data relate to man as a whole: what he is made up of, the various functions that are possible for him (that is, the different forms assumed by his life energy), the relationships between these functions, the states or levels at which these functions operate, the existence of fundamental faculties (attributes of every individual life), certain aspects of these faculties characteristic for man of the levels at which he lives or can live, and the most immediate prospects regarding the various possibilities of his becoming or of his transformation.

Many ways of envisioning man have been put forward by the various systems and philosophies. Most of these have gaps or restricted points of view and interpretations which rob them of any objectivity, and thus render them useless for the study we wish to undertake.

A very ancient knowledge which Gurdjieff makes use of considers that our everyday life is provided for by five functions, each of which has its own "center" or "brain" in which the vital energy takes its appropriate form and in which the use of this energy is controlled in daily life.

Four of these functions are relatively independent and suffice for our daily lives:

the intellectual function, to which all the mental functions belong—formulation of ideas, thinking, and a certain kind of memory, the one with which we are most familiar. It is this function in general which allows us to compare, to judge, to coordinate, to classify and to predict.

the emotional function, which includes all emotion and feeling. It is this function which in general allows us to appreciate and value everything in relation to ourselves (that is, in relationship to what we see and know about ourselves).

the moving function, which includes everything that is a form or a support of the organism and its movement. This is the function which in general allows us to have the sensation of our body and permits the body to accomplish whatever tasks are demanded of it.

the instinctive function, which includes all that regulates and automatically maintains our physical life. It is, in general, by means of this function that we have an instinctive perception of this life's needs.

To differentiate the instinctive function from the moving function, however, is not indispensable at the start. So far as the usual structure is concerned, it is a good enough approximation to take it that one's structure normally consists of three parts or three stories—intellectual, emotional and instinctive-moving.

The fifth function is the sex function, which differs from the others in the sense that it derives support from and participates with the four of them, takes in their emanations and even goes beyond them to be the support of the creative aspect of the human being at every level, with the proper polarity in each case. All our education leads us to think only of the organic aspect of this function. Even from this point of view, we shall soon see that it cannot be studied in isolation. Since the sex function relies on the other functions, the study of these functions must come first, and this brings into our study the entire level of organic life. But sexual polarity and its functioning involves the entirety of the human being, and since this includes levels of life other than the organic level, they also participate in this function. Thus a study of the sex function on the organic level only will result in a partial and inadequate view. A balanced study is not possible until the higher levels of the human being are sufficiently known.

In fact, all the teachings in their various (and sometimes disguised) forms agree in recognizing the possibility for human beings of two higher levels of life. Moreover, ancient knowledge states that in man two more centers exist—two higher centers whose functioning characterizes these levels. But these centers are usually not operating; and, without making a special work, man comes in touch with them only in flashes or not at all. They are: the higher emotional center, to which would belong the only real feelings, and the higher intellectual center, to which would belong an objective form of thinking of which ordinary man has not even an inkling.

The same ancient knowledge to which Gurdjieff invites our attention brings much additional material. It shows that the life of man is spent entirely in three degrees of presence, that is, three levels of functioning or three levels of life: sleep, dreaming and waking. Besides these three states, man sometimes knows for a moment a fourth—the state of self-consciousness. But to these moments of awakening to a state of presence far greater than the one that is usual to him, he practically never gives attention, because he thinks that his presence in the waking state is the fullest and most complete that he is capable of. It satisfies him and is enough for him. He may perhaps seek to improve it, but the idea does not even occur to him that a higher presence is possible for him and could be searched for. Even if he were to suspect its quality, he is not capable of understanding correctly the flashes of self-knowledge given him by certain shocks in life, so long as his attention has not been drawn to what these represent in reality.

Each of these states of presence which are possible for man is, in fact, characterized by the appearance within it of a new "dimension" which does not exist within the underlying levels. Furthermore, these levels are neither destroyed nor lost and may appear at any moment; but they are in a certain sense "transcended" and integrated into a larger whole, where new and different relationships come into being. Because of the appearance of this new "dimension," the passage from one state of presence to another, for the man who experiences it, is marked by a discontinuity, a threshold, an abrupt change, or, to be more precise, a transformation. The functions remain but operate with a different rhythm, with a different amplitude and possibilities inherent in the new relationships and in the coming into play of different centers of activity. And the faculties which are fundamental in all states of presence, participating likewise in this new dimension, are thereby transformed.

In fact, there are three fundamental faculties which are met with under various aspects in every form of individual life, where, taken together, they permit a relatively autonomous individuality, and where their quality is an indicator of the level of life, the state of presence and the degree of being; this quality, varying in accordance with the level, characterizes each state of presence and thus allows it to be recognized and placed. These three faculties, in the case of man, are "attention," "consciousness" and "will." Although man usually ascribes them to himself in a highly developed form, they only exist spontaneously in him in their lower forms, which comprise his ordinary way of life. He only knows their more developed forms accidentally by flashes or when, as a result of a long work on himself, he is able to realize the state of being present to himself. For a man whose states of presence are constantly changing and do not have the permanence that he attributes to them, the fluctuations in the quality of one or another of these three fundamental faculties are important because this makes it possible for him, at each moment, to know the level on which his life is flowing.

These various data are not the only ones that a man can distinguish in himself. In an altogether different order of things, one can recognize that man consists of two parts: one can be called his "essence," the other his "personality." Essence is the inheritance given to man at birth: his physical form, his tendencies, his fundamental characteristics. It is his own property, his inheritance, the bearer of his unique traits, what has been given to him that he might make it bear fruit. And the only real growth of a "man" is the growth of his essence. His personality, on the contrary, is everything that a man has learned: what he has learned since his birth, from the events of his life, from his education, moral upbringing, social environment, and religion. None of that comes from him, all these elements are brought to him, or imposed from the outside; the only thing that may be his own is the manner in which he may have received them as a result of specific traits of his own essence. The first elements of this personality are engraved on what is still virgin ground in earliest infancy and are so deeply lodged in a man that they are even difficult to differentiate from his essence, forming, as it were, a second nature. The future development of an individual depends largely on how these initial data are related to essence. If a fundamental discord has been introduced at this level by the first impressions and the first education received, it becomes deeply buried, and for the individual to be eventually reharmonized this discord has to be found and corrected, difficult though this may be. Later on, the external elements are imprinted less and less deeply.

But as responses to the demands of life are learned, another phenomenon appears—habits are established. Repetition of the same behavior in analogous circumstances creates in an individual a similar association in all his different functions. As a result, a network of special relationships is set up in him, an aspect of his personality, a "way of manifesting" which is automatically reproduced every time certain analogous outer circumstances reappear. Before long, each of these aspects or ways of manifesting constitutes an entity in itself, a particular small "I." An "I" of this kind is formed for each of the habitual circumstances of life, and, as each one is set up independently of the others, there is no connection between them; they are as likely to be in contradiction as in accord, and each is only a partial aspect corresponding to a particular situation. Finally, in life, instead of manifesting himself with an "individuality" in which the functions always express harmoniously what he is in the depth of his essence, a man manifests differently according to circumstances, behind the masks of diverse personages, multiple little "I's" which give him an acquired exterior, foreign to his true self. The whole of this together forms his "personality." But, without the work of self-observation, properly conducted, man obviously has no knowledge of this state of affairs. He believes in the reality of each of these personages; at the moment he believes very "sincerely" that each of them expresses the whole of himself. He does not see his changes and his passages from one character to another and, in general, he believes altogether in his unity.

These observations point up the importance of the relationships which come into existence within ourselves and the necessity of knowing them well.

Attentive observation shows that the five functions on which our everyday life depends are constantly in action but at different degrees of activity; generally, we see that one of them is more active, dominates and leads the others, but this predominance often changes as a result of outer or inner events. There is nevertheless a habitual dominance by one of them, always the same one, according to the type of the individual.

Despite our notion to the contrary and our belief in a degree of freedom within ourselves, correct observation also shows that our functionings are linked together. This dependence—in reality this connection—is evidently very different in each case. Sometimes the connection appears to be so close that it is difficult to separate the functions, owing to our conditionings, our ingrained habits, and, as we have seen, our masks. Sometimes the relationship between different functions is so distant that they appear to be independent of each other and become part of the unconscious, apparently inaccessible to our direct observation.

On the whole, a very great mechanicalness prevails throughout the totality of our ordinary lives, without our even realizing it. Ordinary man is, in fact, a totally conditioned machine, but he does not see it, and if he is told so he does not wish to believe it. The play of associations proceeds in him unceasingly, almost always without his knowledge, in the form of automatic reactions to the situations with which life confronts him. The resulting network, woven out of habits and reproduced every time similar circumstances recur, forms those well-established "ways of being," those masks, which characterize us and which those around us know better than we do. Often they even make use of them; more exactly, they make use of us by means of the unconsciousness in which we are imprisoned.

It is quite obvious that no hope of change or of transformation is open to man as long as he is such a prisoner of his masks and his habits. And if he becomes aware of this, the question arises for him of how to escape. Contrary to what he almost always believes, he cannot escape by himself. Nor can he destroy his habits and his automatic associations because they are necessary in ordinary life. But with the right help, namely, by developing another level within himself, which is the level of the observer or the witness, he can learn to discover them, to know them, and to make use of them. In other words, by developing in himself—through a work of the appropriate kind—a different level of being, this different order of inner relationship can be established without which no liberation would be possible for him.

There is yet another aspect of man that we are asked to envisage as far as this is actually possible for us—namely, the existence and the development of higher bodies. Different religions or teachings tell us that we have, or can have, a soul or an astral body, a causal body, a spirit, a double, and so on. Actually, if we turn our attention toward ourselves, we cannot say that we have had valid objective experiences of this sort; what we have are only intimations, a wish for self-preservation, even for immortality, and some more or less vague premonitions which make us suppose that evolution is actually possible for us in this direction (for example, we speak of "saving" one's soul) and that such an evolution has some relationship either with what becomes of us after physical death or with the inner change for which we have experienced the need. (We speak of going to heaven or purgatory or hell, or, in certain teachings, of reincarnation into conditions better or worse than those of our present lives.) Just as in the organic realm we have a certain instinct which can guide us if the artificiality of our life conditions does not dull it too much, so, in the spiritual realm, we can rediscover a certain "intuition" which can guide us if we know how to make a place for it and to listen. In the Gospels, "man" is a "seed." But no form of life or level of existence is possible without appropriate material support. This is obvious to us on the plane of organic life, which is based on our physical body and on the psychic as well as the instinctive-moving functions. If it is possible for man, through an inner transformation, to reach other levels of life—"higher" or more "subtle" levels—then on these levels also his existence needs a corresponding material support, of similar "subtlety," having its own growth, its own food, its faculties and its functions: this is what is suggested to us and what perhaps we can understand at the beginning about the existence of the higher bodies.

As simplified and schematic as it may be, and even if at first it seems in a certain sense arbitrary, this first collection of data on oneself is necessary as a preliminary sketch on which self-observation can be based. Each new observation, as it is put in its right place on the canvas, reinforces the pattern; but it cannot be analyzed and understood so long as large gaps remain and enough pieces have not been assembled.

Considerable time may be saved if, from the beginning, observation is so directed as to verify the principal and most easily accessible lines of the plan. From this point of view, self-observation must be prepared for by studying the four functions which support our ordinary life, then by studying the different states in which this life is spent, and finally by studying the relationships between the quality of the functions and the different states. Becoming aware of all this as a whole is the first step, and real self-observation cannot come till later.

The conditions, means and significance of real self-observation

LET us now see if we can better understand what self-observation is when it is practised in this way, that is, with the aim of acquiring self-knowledge and approaching the Great Knowledge.

In most traditions, it is said in diverse ways that the Truth is beyond, or within, the world of appearances and that the vision of that Truth liberates man from uncertainty, doubt and conflict. But we certainly feel that before being able to see the inner truth of the world we take part in, the truth about ourselves, it is first of all necessary to resolve these doubts and inner conflicts: we have to begin by learning to turn toward ourselves and to look into ourselves.

Obviously, such a way of seeing oneself, or even the inner movement which makes it possible, is not given to us spontaneously. Again and again we feel ourselves taken by the disorder of outer agitation and find ourselves falling prey to doubts, conflicts and fantasies which stand in the way of an impartial vision of what we are. Once again we must be aware of this and experience a real need to resolve this confusion. For a man finds that these conflicts and this agitation bring with them an impression of life which is hard to give up, and he does not want to see that this agitation is not leading him to anything constructive. So long as he prefers to remain as he is (even if he is not comfortable, since one readily accepts some discomfort), and so long as he does not feel the need to change, absolutely no evolution at all is possible for him.

This need for something to be changed in us is certainly the first observation of ourselves offered by the exigencies of life; sometimes abruptly or brutally and sometimes more gradually as a result of a need, a question or an inner demand. A man's whole wish for a future evolution and the strength of his commitment to it often depend on the quality, the intensity and the force of this observation.

From the moment a man recognizes that there is something wrong or something lacking in him and therefore that something has to be changed, a work on himself can be undertaken toward evolution. And the first question that arises for such a man is how to undertake work which will give him the power really to see himself as he is.

The entire world is seen only in terms of one's self, while this self has no meaning except in terms of the world. At one and the same time we feel ourselves to be the navel of a world which we see from our point of view, while for the world we are nothing—not so much as a speck of dust.

Studying could begin from one side or the other, and our first inclination is to begin with the study of the world around us. But in that world, where we are nothing, we have no capacity either; we have nothing with which to see its eternity or its infinity. We are lost in an immensity beyond our reach and in an analysis which our whole lifetime would not be long enough to encompass, or enable us to complete, in order to synthesize it all. Even if this synthesis could be reached, it would still be necessary to include ourselves within it and find our proper place there. And yet it is just this approach, this endless analysis that modern science has undertaken, with a certain practical efficiency, which has led at the same time to dispersion and specialization, that is, to limitation, without any direct concern for the man who is himself engaged in it.

However, it is we ourselves who are in question in this search; it is we, first and foremost, who need it. It is a matter for us, a matter of our inner being, our place, our conflicts, our evolution, and, from this moment on, of the whole of our life. What is more, for us nothing is seen except through our own eyes.

So, if the study begins with ourselves, it is quite another matter. We are always there, available to ourselves and in the place which we occupy. Perhaps we believe we know ourselves and know this place. Our entire education leads us to think so. Nevertheless, our doubts, our conflicts, and our ignorance are also there: if we knew ourselves as well as we think, these would not exist, and there would be no question about who we are.

We must surely acknowledge that in reality we do not know ourselves. What is more, the mistaken belief that we do know ourselves is the very obstacle which prevents us (since we think it pointless) from undertaking the work which in fact we need the most. If we have some understanding of this situation, we begin to question ourselves about ourselves and we realize that we need to learn to turn ourselves toward ourselves and toward our inner life. We need to see ourselves as we are, instead of the picture we have of ourselves.

To see ourselves better, we must first observe ourselves impartially—in complete sincerity, without changing anything—simply because we have this need to see ourselves as we are. That is why all work in this direction begins with self-observation—observation which is all-embracing, global and impartial.

As soon as we try to observe ourselves in this way and to remain attentive at the same time to ourselves and to a particular aspect of ourselves, we become aware that such an observation is quite fleeting and, except in unusual circumstances, lasts at best only for a few moments.

Very soon, this inability to make the moments of observation last longer seems to us the most important of all the obstacles to knowing oneself, and we begin to wonder why it is usually like this, whether there are special conditions in which it is otherwise, and if so what these conditions are. For someone who commits himself to this path, another kind of difficulty soon arises. Self-observation after a while becomes tedious: after what may have been a certain enthusiasm, the initial interest wanes and any possibility of escape is promptly seized. We forget that the work was undertaken in response to our deepest aspirations and that this waning is an unavoidable stage on the way. We know all this with our head, but our interest, taken by the ever new and changing attractions of life, is constantly allowed to be deflected. If I do not feel that for myself I am a question that never leaves me in peace, if this question no longer awakes a real interest in myself, if I do not feel a sense of self-betrayal—or more exactly that I sacrifice the highest possibility for my development—when I allow myself to be completely taken by the current of outer life, then why should I undertake such a search? No effort of inner work, no attempt at self-observation has any meaning whatever unless each attempt is connected to our original search and with our wish to be more fully ourselves.

But even if this interest in ourselves can be awakened, the fact remains that the attempt to observe oneself does not last longer than a few moments. At one and the same time we see that our actual interest in our attempts is exhausted and that the attention necessary for seeing is soon used up. What we observe vanishes very quickly, and, such as we are, we certainly have to confess that we constantly forget ourselves and that we forget ourselves all the time. Forgetting, and especially forgetting oneself, immediately appears as one of the most difficult obstacles to overcome for the man who is searching to be himself. In these conditions no self-observation can really be useful. Thus we are compelled to study why our observations are so transient and how they could be sustained long enough for valid findings to become possible for us. It becomes evident that a great deal of preliminary work is necessary.

Right self-observation, leading to valid findings, requires and is, in fact, dependent upon the participation of three factors, one might say three forces; and the quality of the result, that is to say, the quality of the observation, depends on the quality of each of these three factors. They are: I who observe, face to face with what I observe within myself; and nothing takes place unless a third factor is also there between them, namely an attention which connects the two.

The attention which is needed here is no doubt just what we lack the most; it is a particular kind of attention which we do not usually have and up till now we did not know it was possible. The attention we ordinarily have is a one-way attention directed toward what we observe and taking nothing but that into account. With this kind of attention and the attitude that goes with it, observation applied to oneself makes it possible to arrive at a rudimentary analysis (as in classroom psychology), but not to have those observations of a particular part or aspect together with the whole of ourselves which we are searching for. The attention we need is an attention from another level, which at the same time as observation is going on takes into account everything that we are. It is a two-way attention, an attention divided in two, and it entails an attitude that is very different from our usual one. We do not naturally have any of this kind of attention except accidentally in certain moments of surprise or danger when it is part of a flash of consciousness. But it is possible for us "artificially," through a special effort, and it can be developed in us through appropriate exercises. This is one of the results of attempting to observe oneself. To begin with, our attention remains one way, goes now in one direction, now in another, sometimes toward myself, sometimes toward what I observe in myself, alternating at a faster or slower speed. And this happens as easily in one direction as in another; in the beginning there is no stable support on which our attention can be based. Real self-observation, if we attempt it, soon appears to us to depend as much on this support as on the attention itself. And we understand very quickly that the three factors, the three forces that must be present, are closely interdependent.

So to understand better what a real observation is we come to take into account the two other factors, those which confront each other in this effort: I who observe and what I observe in myself.

Real self-observation, as we understand it, is only possible if the one who observes—"I"—is present while the observation is going on; the integration of what is observed will be the more valid and complete the more the one who observes is present, that is, able to take account, in the field of attention directed toward himself, of a greater number of elements. This presupposes that he already recognizes these elements and is able to keep them together there with some stability, which can be called keeping oneself in a state of being present to oneself. This state is not a natural one for us but it too can be developed by a work of self-study, and each time it arises in us we recognize it by a special inner consciousness, a special inner sense of self which, once it has been experienced, is unmistakable.

Nothing of all this is possible for us at the beginning. These moments of presence, even if they appear in us when we are under certain influences, are brief and separated by long intervals, often entire days, when we live as we usually do in a dispersed state without the knowledge of what we are as a whole. We must admit that we forget ourselves almost uninterruptedly. In us, things do themselves—speaking, laughing, feeling, acting—but they do it automatically and we ourselves are not there. One part laughs, another speaks, another acts. We do not feel: I speak, I act, I laugh, I observe. Nothing that is done in this way can be integrated into a whole. We live in self-forgetfulness, and it all happens without leaving any trace. Life lives itself, but there is no "fruit" for the one who lives it.

Self-observation is useless if just any observer can take my place and if "I," the subject, am not there to understand while observation is going on. Complete and true self-observation would require the overall presence of a real and stable I. Such a presence is not possible for man without a long work of self-knowledge; but a relative degree of presence, a certain coherence of all that he can collect in himself is possible even now, at any moment, through an effort of "self-remembering." Only if we try to make this effort at the same time can real self-observation begin. In trying it, we discover, moreover, that without it we are constantly changing and that all that we have collected is dispersed at the slightest chance distraction. In practice, nothing is more difficult for us than to be there with enough stability for an observation.

The remaining factor which enters into self-observation is that which I observe in myself. This is the object and support of our observation, which would be impossible if this support also were constantly disappearing from view. If we look for this kind of stable support in ourselves we can very soon realize that what is easiest to see, our exterior, that is, the form of our responses to the demands of life, depends first of all on the demands themselves and, even if it can be repeated, only indirectly on ourselves. It is constantly changing and, in fact, escapes us altogether.

On the other hand, the functional structures which allow us to respond are always there, invariably the same in all circumstances, the result of what we are and what life has made them. But such as they are, these structures (our functions, our personalities) are not usable. The way things take place in us, the interaction of our functions and the manner in which they associate to produce our personalities and responses, all this goes on in the dark without our knowing it. And what we are ordinarily cannot come within sight of our observations unless we do something "special" to make it visible.

It is definitely not possible to arrive at the kind of observation needed for our search unless the three active factors which allow observation to take place appear simultaneously—an "I" who observes, the field observed in a complete moment of life, and the two-way attention which relates them.

The easiest and most dependable of the special conditions which make this kind of work possible are the different forms of struggle against the automatic aspects of myself: those personages are always there. All disciplines for the development of man, whatever they are and whether the form given to them is obvious or not, begin with this kind of struggle. It is a necessity which accords with the general laws of the evolution of life.

Observation with a view to self-knowledge can be no exception to this law. It begins, on the simplest level, by a struggle against the usual fetters (that is, habits) which make us appear as what we seem to be. This struggle, because of its uselessness in the immediate present, because of its inability to change whatever is there—and the mistake of expecting it to—and because of the persistence and energy it calls for, is tedious, difficult and irksome. No man could conceive of undertaking it unless he has understood what it is leading to and unless he remembers constantly why he is undertaking it. But if he has reached such an understanding, or even, at the beginning, if he has understood that it is necessary for him to submit to this discipline, then the struggle against habits becomes at once an obvious means to see himself as he is, and, without his being able to be aware of it, the first instrument for achieving his inner transformation. It arouses this double attention which he needs and forces him to confront these habits which keep him asleep, automatized, and engulfed in constant self-forgetfulness.

Our habits and, when they are more firmly rooted in us, our unconscious conditionings, are innumerable. They are so tightly entangled that they are inextricable, and from this point of view it could be said that ordinary man is not a well-woven cloth (except perhaps in his instinctive part), but a haphazard patchwork of habits and conditionings, both small and large.

To start with, for the struggle with habits to be possible and profitable for self-observation, we need to choose simple habits, directly related to functions which have already been clearly recognized.

The study of the moving part is undoubtedly the easiest. While a man cannot make direct observations in the usual way for more than moments at a time, observation can be effectively carried out by going against one after another of the various moving habits which form the substratum of all our activity—the way we walk, write, our gestures at the table or in our profession, postures, and so forth. Each is made up of many small habits, which if altered intentionally can serve as a support for self-observation. The length of one's step, the style of walking, the way of holding a pen, the way of using one hand instead of another are examples which can be multiplied indefinitely. At the same time, a man who practices self-observation quickly perceives that he is confined without knowing it in a rather limited number of moving habits; and this in itself is quite important.

The study of intellectual functioning is somewhat more difficult. A man who tries to see this functioning notices that he does have a certain power to direct his thoughts at the start; he can sometimes keep them for a little while in the direction he has chosen. But, sooner or later, often quite soon, they escape him and he is distracted. Besides, in his ordinary life, he seldom makes use of his power to direct his thoughts except in rare moments; his mind never stops working and ideas are always there, arising automatically as a result of outer and inner stimuli about which a man can do nothing. They are automatic reactions of the intellect in various conditions which follow one after another in a chain of associations. And in the same way that we have physical habits, so do we have habits of the mind, habitual ways of thinking which, without our knowing it, are also rather few in number.

One of the first lines of study of the intellectual function is the struggle with these habitual ways of thinking. A man can become aware that each particular way in which he thinks is not the only one. He can question them and he can make himself look for other ways of thinking, deepen them, understand them, and understand in what sense they are not his own ways. Proceeding thus, he will make some valuable discoveries about himself and his way of thinking.

Another line of study of intellectual functioning is the observation of ourselves when being distracted. It is a clear indication of the deficiency of our intellectual center. We begin to read, talk, listen, then suddenly we are distracted. If we do not wish to be constantly distracted from the aims we have decided to pursue, we need to know what takes place in us and how such distraction occurs. Attentive observation—and this is difficult because the process is subtle—shows us two principal causes: imagination and dreaming. Both are examples of the wrong functioning of the intellectual center and of its laziness, owing to which it tries to spare itself all the efforts which effective work would require, a work that is going in a definite direction toward a well-defined aim.

Imagination exists in each one of our centers in a form peculiar to it. It follows closely on a moment of real work having a definite direction, after which the effort weakens, the attention deviates, the aim is lost sight of, and the functioning continues within the center itself without any connection whatever with the work which was undertaken or any connection with the other centers, except for bringing in useless and aimless—that is, imaginary—impressions of life, made up purely for satisfying the function and not for effective expression in the realm of reality. One center or several centers may take part in elaborations of this nature, which turn a man aside from the tasks imposed on him by life, and act, more or less, as a substitute for them.

Fantasy and daydreaming are the opposite of a useful activity of the mind, that is to say, one linked to a well-determined aim. To observe and know them a man has to undertake to struggle against them by restricting himself to tasks which are precise, concrete and clearly defined.

Once he has undertaken this struggle he soon notices that daydreaming is always a useless form of dreaming, understandable at a pinch when it brings pleasant sensations but morbid and self-destructive when it moves to negative and depressing associations of which self-pity is the most usual. A man also notices that the value usually given to imagination is in no way justified, for it is a destructive faculty which he can never control. It carries him away in unforeseeable directions unrelated to his conscious aims. He begins to imagine something for the pleasure of it, then very soon begins to believe, at least partly, in what he is imagining and allows himself to be carried away. This kind of imagination is in no way that creative faculty rightly regarded as of incalculable worth. It is, in fact, pernicious, merely a degenerate caricature of a higher faculty, that of real creative imagination, or conscious prefiguration in conformity with an objective knowledge of data and laws, which ordinary man does not possess. But with fantasies and daydreaming man deludes himself that he possesses this higher faculty. If he observes himself impartially he becomes aware of this illusion and that he is lying to himself, and he understands that in fact daydreams and imagination are among the principal obstacles to self-observing and seeing himself as he is. Nothing is more painful for a man; it is, symbolically, the fall of Icarus.

A third line of our intellectual functioning, which in this case concerns joint functioning of the intellect and other centers, is observation of our habit of talking for talking's sake.

Spoken language is intellectual material picked up in social life and inscribed in the moving center, an instrument put by this center at the disposal of all the others so that they can express themselves and communicate through it. It is necessary to speak and express oneself—life is an exchange; but besides responding to this necessity, talking very quickly becomes a habit. It becomes a habit from infancy, when small children are taught to talk for the sake of talking and not to express themselves. Later we are even taught to speak brilliantly about everything and about nothing. And we do not even realize that this is how we are. Little needs to be said, but we speak a lot. Talking can even become a vice. There are people who never stop talking—about anything, everywhere, all the time, even in their sleep, and if nobody else is there they talk to themselves.

To struggle with this habit of talking, which we all have in one degree or another, is also an excellent means of self-observation available to us at all times; the rule of silence is part of certain monastic disciplines. Struggling with the habit of talking and against all unnecessary words forces us to see what it is that arises in us and uses language, and in this way we may collect important observations as to what we are made of.

Study of the emotional function, even arrived at indirectly by way of our habitual emotional habits, is probably even more difficult than study of the intellectual center, for as soon as we try to observe it we have to admit that we have no hold on it. We can change nothing as regards our emotions. Although they are always there, we see them only when they are stronger than usual. Then we call them "feelings." But a real feeling would be something quite different. We live with nothing but automatic emotional reactions, feelings which follow each other in rapid succession at each instant of our lives and cause something in each circumstance to please us or displease us, attract us or repel us. We no more see this than we know why we experience our attractions and repulsions, our acceptances and refusals; they take place in us automatically. A man who wishes to observe himself sees this only by flashes, and in such moments of seeing he is, in general, disagreeably surprised. He has no desire whatever to prolong the experience, and if he forces himself to do so, it may give rise to deep repercussions in him, some of which may be dangerous, for we set great store by these automatic emotional reactions. A right observation of our habitual emotional functioning puts in question everything that I am and obliges me to see what the values which I hold to, and in whose name I live, stand for. This touches on the very possibilities of man's evolution. To undertake such work without altering or destroying these possibilities forever, a "feeling" of quite another order has first to have been awakened.

There is, however, one area in which a man who wishes to observe himself runs no risk. He can engage in a struggle with emotional habits that will show him a whole side of his habitual emotional functioning—this struggle is the attempt not to express unpleasant emotions. He who observes himself very soon notices that he is unable to observe anything impartially; this is particularly true for what he sees in himself, but also for what he sees outside himself. About every single thing, he has a personal "feeling": "I don't care," "I like it," or "I dislike it." But whereas he can easily refrain from expressing his agreement or indifference, it is almost impossible for him not to express his disapproval in one way or another. This easily becomes a habit and is often even taken as a sign of sincerity. The negative impression received in such a case is expressed in some form of violence, contentiousness or depression—anger, jealousy, fault-finding, suspicion, worry, fear, self-pity, and so on. In all these forms some expression of personal negativity replaces the simple expression which flows from just noting the facts as they are. These forms bear witness to my inability to keep my personal grievances to myself and to a tendency to let them gush out over my surroundings so as not "to feel alone"—to make others share them and to try to get rid of them in that way. This is both a sign of my own weakness, my incapacity to accept myself and things as they are, and an enormous and useless waste of energy which I impose also on those near me in a chain reaction which spreads and multiplies the negativity. Now this is one of the few emotional processes which can be cut short without risk of harmful consequences. Brought to bear on the expression of negative emotions (for it is their outer expression which needs to be restrained and not the emotions themselves), this struggle in no way upsets the inner equilibrium. It only involves the saving of a considerable amount of energy which would have been totally lost if spent externally but which, being saved in this way, can be used for other purposes. At the same time, it allows the observer to discover in himself an entirely new aspect of the emotional process with which he lives.

Thus, the struggle against automatic habits established in each of our centers can be a support for the early stages of self-observation, just as later another kind of struggle—of oneself with oneself (between the two aspects of man)—will be necessary to serve as a basis for the appearance of a "presence," and later still the struggle between the yes and the no (that is, between the two natures of man) will be necessary for his spiritualization. The story of the liberation of man is one of constant struggle against increasingly subtle forms of mechanicalness, and it all begins on the level of habits by a struggle to arrive at real self-observation.

By practicing self-observation in this way, a man will notice that it brings about a change in his inner life, and in the processes that flow from it.

Self-observation as we have tried it requires an inner division. For observation to be possible, a certain separation between two parts of oneself has to be established. Immediately the question arises about myself: "who observes and who is observed?" And at the same time, this separation brings about the beginning of consciousness, an awareness under which "I" begin to wonder who is really myself, what is "sincere" and what is not. With this inner awareness and the light it projects, the processes that till now took place in complete darkness appear for what they are and are again put in question in relation to what I discover to be me. And this sincere questioning, continuous in the light of an expanding self-consciousness, is the very ferment that will make possible all further changes. Self-observation is in itself an instrument for awakening to another level of life and, consequently, a means of transformation. In fact, without his knowing it, the man who observes himself hastens the appearance in him of the three forces, which, together and independently, are the first intimation of a stable self-development—that is, the development of an individuality endowed with an autonomous presence.

What these "changes" will be is perhaps not at all what the man who observes himself might at first think.

To the extent that he observes himself and his self-knowledge increases, he gradually becomes aware how completely mechanical his ordinary life is and how totally powerless he is in the face of it, so that no direct change is possible for him. These mechanical processes are what they are and neither observing them nor analyzing them can bring anything more.

Little by little he understands that any change in these processes can never be more than a limited one, and that real change, or rather transformation, can come to him only by going beyond these ordinary processes through the development of an inner being that will be truly himself.

From this moment on, an entirely new question appears and the work takes on a new meaning—to foster this growth of another being within him. It is then no longer enough to see himself in the way he tried before. With the first intimation of self-knowledge having gradually replaced the simplest kind of self-observation, the intimation of presence to oneself takes the place of the earlier reminders to remember oneself. The far-off vision becomes an observation of oneself by oneself.

He who observes himself in this way quickly comes to see that as he ordinarily lives, he himself (that is, his personality) is the worst enemy of his self (that is, his essence, his being). This is precisely what is wrong with us as we are, the major obstacle to being ourselves. Personality, built up by the environment in which we live, constantly interferes, and prevents the expression of our being. The functions, supported by the body, are at the service of the personages that we have acquired, and not of our inner being, our real self, which can no longer make itself heard.

But it is necessary to be certain of this, as the result of much impartial observation and innumerable constatations which leave no room for doubt. Nothing is more tenacious than the false picture we have of ourselves, and it takes a long time, many self-deceptions and many sincere observations, before a man begins to understand this and see himself as he is.

When real seeing appears, he understands that everything has to be turned upside down. If, instead of an all-powerful personality making free with the functions without any concern for his very weak being, a man really wishes to be himself, it is his own being which has to be reoriented and developed until it is able to take the primary place. It must take over direction of the functions liberated from the dominance of the person, and make use at will of the personages which up till then had usurped its place.

When this vision of himself appears, a man begins to understand the meaning of real work on himself and glimpses the first stage of his possible evolution.

States of presence

THE states in which man lives—more precisely, states of presence—can be viewed as the "dimensions" of his life, the different levels of activity at each of which the individual's life admits of different possibilities.

In the different states which are possible for him, the individual exists with his various constituent parts. But the development of these various parts, their mutual relationships, and the quality of their functioning change. Throughout the range of states, the structure stays the same, but the quality of life changes.

Man can live in four states, which are usually classified by their relative degree of consciousness, since this is the faculty whose changes are the easiest to see.

Although man's structure stays the same, it takes on a characteristic aspect in each of these states. A certain degree of "presence," resulting from all this, is inherent in each of these states. This presence finds material support in a body, or perhaps, several bodies, which give it a structure and a means of manifestation. It also has a spiritual support, appropriate to its own level, from the standpoint of the three fundamental being-factors: consciousness, attention and will, which are in turn reflections of three great fundamental creative forces: active, reconciling and receptive. A man's presence also has seven centers, each of which has a brain as its chief support. Each of these centers has specific qualities, which together constitute what is innate in every man—his own essence. The corresponding function depends on each center and brain; and the functions as a whole, with their various levels of operation, connections and relationships, express every man's individuality or make up the form of his personality.

Nothing in man can be understood and no self-knowledge is possible if the different states are not taken into account.

For a completely evolved man four states of presence are possible. But an ordinary man lives in only two of these, the lowest, with flashes of the third. He may have theoretical information concerning the fourth state, but in actuality the two higher states are inaccessible to him; he is incapable of understanding them and judges what he knows of them from the perspective of the lower states he lives in, which falsify his valuation of them.

The first state is sleep, a passive state in which man can do nothing except regenerate his energy. A third of his life, sometimes even a half, is spent in this state of passive consciousness, filled only with dreams which he himself considers unreal.

The second state is the waking state, a state which man takes to be active, and in which he spends the other half of his life. He moves around, decides, does business, talks politics, crushes or kills his neighbor, discusses lofty subjects, and fathers children, all in this state which he calls his waking, or clear, state of consciousness. However, it is nothing but a caricature, and even the slightest impartial study shows at once that this waking state is passive, and that in it man is utterly lacking in clarity. He is, at the very best, in a state of "relative" consciousness.

The third state of presence is the state of self-consciousness, or consciousness of one's own being. In this state man sees himself as he is and becomes objective toward himself. It is, properly speaking, the state of "subjective" consciousness. Usually it is assumed that man possesses this state, and indeed, by the fact of his being three-centered by nature, it should be his natural right. But, due to the abnormal conditions of his existence (in which he constantly mistakes his dreams for reality), not only does he not have access to this state, but he is not even aware of its absence. Ordinary man has it only in flashes and fails even to appreciate the significance of them.

The fourth state of presence is the state of "objective" consciousness. In this state a man could come in touch with the real objective world (which he is separated from by his senses, his dreams and his subjective states of consciousness), and thus he could see and perceive things as they are. But this state is not given him by nature and can come only as the end result of a process of inner transformation and of a long work on himself. As in the case of self-consciousness, ordinary man has only flashes of objective consciousness, which he does not even notice and can remember only when he is in the state of self-consciousness. But ordinary man has a great deal of theoretical information about this fourth state on the basis of which he imagines he is able to reach it directly. Quite apart from fraud and charlatanism, every religion includes descriptions and accounts of what it calls ecstacy, enlightenment, and so on. And man often sets out in search of this without understanding that the only right way toward objective consciousness leads through the development of self-consciousness. Moreover, it is one of the characteristics of the state of ordinary consciousness (the second state) that the authentic knowledge which it can contain is constantly mixed with dreams and imagination which in the end submerge it.

A fully developed man, a man in the full sense of the word, should possess these four states of consciousness; but ordinary people live in only two states. Just as, in the state of sleep, they can have only glimmers of relative consciousness, so also, in the state of relative consciousness, they can have only glimmers of self-consciousness. If a man wants to have longer periods of self-consciousness and not just glimmers, he has to understand that they cannot come by themselves. First he must see that he is a prisoner in a subjective world, made up of dreams and fantasies which screen reality from him. Then he has to undertake a long work to free himself from dreams and to awake to this reality, first in himself and afterward in the life outside him. More than anything, we must understand that, even in the waking state, we are asleep (the real "I" is asleep) and that what we need above all else is to awaken, that is to say, to undertake the work that is necessary for awakening the real I.

Always remembering the need for progressive verification by our own experience, perhaps we can now try to understand better, theoretically, what the four possible states are and what information can be gathered about them.

The first and lowest state of consciousness for us is sleep. It is a passive and purely subjective state in which we are almost entirely cut off from the outer world and plunged into an inner world where there is no awareness. We are surrounded by dreams; the psychic functions work without direction, independently of one another. Purely subjective images—echoes of past experiences or echoes of vague perceptions in the present (sounds, sensations, smells), or far-off echoes of a deeper level of life—pass through the mental apparatus, leaving only faint traces in the memory or, more often, no trace at all.

Sleep is, however, a very important state. Aside from the fact that man spends a third of his time in it, it is the state in which his organic nature—like everything endowed with organic life—restores the energies needed for existence in the waking state. It can be said that sleep recharges the accumulators of energy associated with the centers (which we will study in detail in the next chapter).

The presence of man in the state of sleep is purely passive, and all the more so according to the depth of his sleep (for in man there are various levels of sleep). The body is more or less reduced to its instinctive functionings—completely so in the deepest sleep.

The centers with their particular features—the inner being of man—are there, but either receive no impressions at all or else do not respond to any that do by chance reach them. Even if one of them does occasionally respond, this leads to no associated response from the other functions. Only the instinctive center functions fully, freed (at least in deepest sleep) from any other influence or connected only with the corresponding instinctive-motor parts of the other centers.

During sleep, though the instinctive functions operate fully and freely, the other functions are at rest, and the associations between them, depending on the depth of sleep, are more or less completely disconnected from each other. Because of this the two "energy accumulators" attached to each of the centers (which we will study later) are not called on to supply any energy other than for the instinctive work, and the centers are therefore free to tap directly the central source of being-energy, by means of which they communicate with each other. A free circulation of energy is established, and when nothing happens to disturb it (as in deep sleep), the reserves of the specific energy required by each of the centers and the balance between these energies are restored without hindrance.

In fact, however, there are many intermediate states between the waking state and the state of deep sleep, the true sleep. What characterizes sleep is that the centers are disconnected from one another, and at the same time their ability to manifest is suspended. But in ordinary man most often these disconnections are incomplete. Since ordinary man lives in five centers, any one of the five may or may not be disconnected. His sleep is usually an intermediate state in which one or several of the connections, but not all, are broken. Sleep generally begins with the disconnection of the thinking center, that is, the ordinary mental activity we live with; this is what we customarily call going to sleep. But it is not always this way; one or more of the other parts may be cut off while the mental activity goes on. In general, however, such intermediary states are not recognized as sleep, and according to current notions the disconnection of the mental faculties is what differentiates the waking states from sleep.

The center which is disconnected next, or at the same time as the thinking center, is the moving center. Man and most animals lie down to sleep. Then the other centers are disconnected, but not always. In fact, many modes of disconnection are possible; the breaks and the order in which they occur depend on individual habits and circumstances. One can sleep standing up, walk in one's sleep, make love in one's sleep, talk in one's sleep, and so on. At the opposite extreme is the instinctive center, which is the last to be disconnected, and, what is more, is never disconnected without special—and dangerous—work and even then (as long as life lasts) only at certain of its levels, for complete and definitive disconnection leads to organic death.

Although constitutional predispositions often enter in, all this is subject to constant change—a sleep-walker, for example, neither walks in his sleep every night, nor all night long.

The state of deep sleep has a significance and importance which ordinary man does not as a rule suspect. In ancient traditions, the Hindu tradition in particular, it occupies a major place as a state in which the subject no longer experiences any desire and has not a single dream, and thus may be regarded as a return to the primordial state of serenity. The being (the essence) withdraws into the primordial formless realm—the source of future manifestations in the other states—where, all conflict of form having died down, it enjoys in "bliss" (*Ananda*) the fullness of itself and returns in itself to the realm of pure being (*Ishwara*). In this state the different modes of manifestation, including those proper to its individuality, are not annihilated, but remain potentially in the integral whole of all possibilities, in which the individual being has rejoined universal Essence. Because it keeps enough consciousness of its own possibilities, it retains a connection with its form of being and is able to return to its own way of manifesting in the realm of form. This connection, however, may be lost during certain school exercises related to deep sleep: that is one of the risks of such exercises. Fully developed beings can consciously break this connection when they choose. We are told that they know, or choose, the moment of their physical death.

Thus, deep sleep can be understood as a return to the state of pure "essentiality," analogous to the embryonic state (at the beginning of individual life) of the essence, increased by such development of essence as has been attained up until then through life experience. And in such a state an individual man, having returned to the confines of universal, non-individual, unmanifested Being, enters there into resonance with the essential life forces which re-equilibrate and regenerate him.

But this return to the fundamental forces of Life in pure Essence, complete Bliss and perfect Harmony is entirely passive as regards the individual; it takes place through the abandonment of all manifestation of his own and all expression of his individuality—apart from the survival of the instinctive organic function, that is, the automatic life of the body. In deep sleep the three principal faculties from which the individual derives his quality of presence and his power of manifestation (that is, attention, consciousness and will—reflections of the three fundamental creative forces) are completely suspended. A man in a state of deep sleep no longer exercises any of these powers and they remain only "potential."

Although the state of deep sleep is in fact analogous to that of full Realization (the fourth state, or the state of objective consciousness), with fullness of Being (essence as well as manifestation), full Knowledge (and not only Bliss), and perfect Serenity (and not simply Harmony), which are included in this Realization, these two states are nevertheless at the opposite poles of life. The state of deep sleep extends to the boundaries of states of infra-individual Being (to the boundaries of pure Substance), and the state of full Realization extends to the boundaries of states of supra-individual Being (to the boundaries of pure Spirit). Between the two, the states possible for man range from the darkness of substance to the light of pure consciousness. No other form of being, in the world known to us, is endowed with, and responsible for, such possibilities.

In the intermediate states of sleep, dream "phenomena" are produced. Deep sleep brings about an inhibition of all the functions of the centers and at the same time interrupts the connections with the memory and imagination in each of them. But if they are not disconnected, or only partly disconnected, these functions may go on working in their respective centers. And thus the machine is not completely at rest, and some traces of its functioning may be available to us in the waking state. Study of these traces, that is, the study of dreams, can then tell us something both in regard to those disturbances which were strong enough to prevent the machine from resting (which of the connections are not properly broken) and also as to the nature of the disturbance in question (its causes and significance).

Theoretically, dreams can be divided into three principal categories: associative (or reactive) dreams, compensatory dreams and symbolic (or archetypal) dreams. But there are many other kinds, such as premonitory dreams, or telepathic dreams, the significance of which it would be interesting to examine from the point of view of the breaking or non-breaking of the connections between centers.

Inevitably, one tends to relate the three principal categories of dreams to the three levels of ordinary human life: associative dreams correspond to mechanical life, compensatory dreams correspond to a personal aspect colored by emotion, while symbolic dreams may offer obscure glimpses into the life of the real self, when the higher emotional center (working on another level) is able to make itself felt, owing to a sufficient disconnection between the lower centers, which ordinarily hide it.

In any case, dreams in sleep are still a subjective phenomenon. Even when induced by certain external impressions, they are formed in the inner world of a man and are made up of elements contained within him. Seeing them in the waking state, if he can recall them, a man may not recognize the images which were used as his own and may feel them as foreign to him. Yet this is nothing but an optical illusion: even though he does not know it, they are in him and pertain to him, whatever form they may assume and however alien they may appear. They are only various aspects of himself arising in himself, ultimately indicative of things contained in him which he did not know of.

In a man whose development is incompletely realized, who is unbalanced due to the disharmony of his centers, the disconnections either take place wrongly or not at all. Aside from purely associative or reactive dreams (the mechanical dreams induced by perceptions), dreams indicative of a more essential suffering may occur, signifying something missing or unbalanced in the life of the essence, and a tendency for this lack to be satisfied in various forms by dreaming.

On the contrary, in a man whose daily activity is complete, harmonized, and fully "satisfying," the disconnection of the various centers on going to sleep takes place harmoniously, progressively, completely, and apparently without dreams, that is, without an abrupt break, and without impressions different enough from those of the waking state, or strong enough, for him to be able to remember them.

In the case of a man who has attained the third state of consciousness—the state of presence to oneself and self-consciousness—on going to sleep he begins by deactivating the connections he has established between the higher emotional center and the ordinary centers. This he does consciously and by the exercise of will. Such a man goes to sleep intentionally when he sees fit. Just as in the case of a man whose ordinary activity is harmonious, the disconnection in sleep of the lower centers is complete, takes place smoothly and without dreams that can be remembered. But at the same time the contact with the higher self is not lost. It remains linked with its support, and, though no longer expressing itself through that medium, is still vigilant, and thanks to it the alternation of sleep and waking is analogous to what the alternation of breathing in and breathing out is for the lower self: this movement for the I, between sleep and waking, is, or should be, "organic" life and death.

The second of the states of consciousness possible for man is the waking state. It appears of itself when he emerges from sleep and is the state in which he works, speaks, acts, thinks and dreams. It is at the same time less passive and more "subjective" than sleep, and in it he makes a distinction between himself and what is not himself, between his body and objects which are not his body, objects which he knows by their qualities and position and which he can make use of. He becomes aware of a duality—and a latent opposition—between himself and the world. In this state he says that he has an "awakened consciousness" or a "clear consciousness," and he attributes to it many qualities not present in sleep.

Actually, the only difference between sleep, with its various degrees, and the ordinary waking state is that the mental apparatus, that is, the mechanical part of the intellectual function, which reacts and associates automatically, is reconnected. The role of this formatory apparatus is to link together and coordinate the impressions received by the different centers. All the characteristics of sleep remain, and a man's presence in this waking state is no more than a higher level of sleep in which each of the centers is reconnected to the mental apparatus that has again become active. But the higher centers remain disconnected, and the I goes on sleeping; the lower centers are still cut off from one another, and no direct confrontation is set up between them, with the result that each goes on with its own imagining. These dreams which go on in the centers converge at the level of the automatic mind with the impressions that the centers receive from life: sensory perceptions, emotions and desires. Dream and reality are inextricably mixed and the automatic mind is unable to discriminate between them. It merely confronts, associates, records and balances all the material that comes to its notice, without any other grounds than its own activity for classifying and evaluating them. The arising in the mental apparatus of impressions of approval or disapproval, agreement or contradiction, possibility or impossibility, produces an impression of life in which the inner material coming from dreams, imagination and automatic thought (perceptive and associative) occupy the same place and are of the same, if not more, importance as the real interior and exterior perceptions of the moment. The effect of these new impressions is that the mental apparatus, now active again, sends toward each of the centers the impulses that result from its associations; they are the responses of the mental apparatus to the requirements of the moment, and these mental responses, in which the centers play no direct part, constantly substitute for the responses of the real I, which is asleep. The result is that the mental apparatus on its own takes on an appearance of reality and continuity; and it assumes an illusory personality which takes the place of real individuality, that of the I. But in his waking state a man no more understands this than he understands the waking state while he is asleep. So long as his real I is asleep, he cannot understand that the authority and the decisions of his mental apparatus are those of a usurper.

However, if he is willing to see himself mercilessly as he is (but of course he must also be given the means to do so), the facts oblige him to recognize that such a state cannot be considered lucid in any effective sense.

His presence in the waking state is apparently active—it is in any case full of activity. But this activity is in fact only reaction: automatic mental reactions to information received and to knowledge recorded. The functions react automatically according to reflexes acquired under the influence of the surrounding world—the education received, the established habits. This "life" is entirely reactive and associative; it may remain purely functional or take place under the domination of one or other of the centers in turn, but it never requires their participation together as one whole; that is, the essence, with the real I, in fact receives nothing, plays no part, remains asleep, does not live, and does not grow. The real I is disconnected from it all. From the point of view of a real I and real individuality, the waking state is a passive state. The incessant activity of the functions makes life possible, but this activity goes on in the sleep and passivity of the I.

Thus in their waking state, people actually live asleep, in the sleep of the I. They do not yet know anything about this I. They do not know they are asleep, and they do not see that everything they do consists of unconscious reactions under the influence of the dreams and external forces which fashion and direct their mental apparatus, and by means of it make use of them, without their knowledge and without their being aware of it. They live in sleep without knowing it and do not understand that the first thing they have to do is to wake up, that is, succeed at any cost in awakening their I. Many ancient teachings, and particularly the Gospels, warn man that he has to awaken. But the real meaning of these ideas is rarely understood, and for men of the present day there are very great obstacles in the way of an exact view of their situation.

The quality of daily life, activities and behavior thus remains entirely reactive, and the three great fundamental faculties which might provide meaning only exist there as yet in a reflected form: a fragmentary consciousness (only in one center or dominated by one center) changing from moment to moment; a dispersed attention moving from one thing to another or on the contrary caught by some "fascinating" aspect; a "will" that is constantly weakening or taking the form of sporadic whims. Finally, a variety of personages occupy the stage, all made up of the same familiar collection of qualities and functions, but differing in each case in their number and proportion: now in constant change, now held captive by some idea or some fixed emotion, they are always without any direct relation to what could be a stable and permanent I.

But man does not spontaneously see this state, and even if he is told about it, it is the last thing he is willing to accept. When the facts of life make it obvious, he immediately finds some explanation (a good excuse or what may perhaps be better called a "buffer") which allows him to go on with his dream and to continue taking himself for what he is not.

Yet such a state is worse than sleep. A man asleep is entirely passive and can do nothing. In the waking state, on the contrary, a man can act, and the results of his so-called conscious actions have a repercussion on himself and his environment.

More serious still are the obstacles which make it impossible to see what the situation is. The chief obstacle, from which all the others are derived, is undoubtedly the fact that in his waking state man does not see that he is asleep and has forgotten his real self.

He does not see it even when it is pointed out to him because he has no idea what could be his "self": he does not know himself and, for better or worse, is satisfied with his present state. He has very little useful information about himself: in its place there are dreams and imagination. Dreams and imagination about what one is and what life is are two other major obstacles. The power of imagination in particular keeps a man in a constant state of actual hypnosis in which the false ideas which he invents about himself, and the self-love with which he defends them, prevent him from ever having a chance to see himself as he is. Many other features inherent in the present-day life of man help to keep him in this situation. And if by some happy accident (which may very well never take place) the shock of events forces him to question, if only for an instant, the abnormal way in which he himself and his life have been built up, the automatic mechanism of excuses and buffers immediately provides means, in the form of justification and explanations, to cease having any question about himself, but only about other people or circumstances that do not depend upon him.

Lastly, in this state a man has none of those properties that he so readily attributes to himself: unity in himself and, in life, clear consciousness, will, freedom, the ability to do.

Actually, in this state in which he constantly forgets himself, man does not know what he is. He lets himself be taken along in the play of passing events, either, when they are to his liking, identifying with them and being carried away, or, when he finds them unpleasant, resisting them and getting lost in the resistance. Forgetting oneself, identification, opposition to people and circumstances, fallacious and fantastic imagination about oneself protected by an easily aroused vanity: such are the characteristics of this waking state in which man's life usually unfolds without his finding anything, anywhere, that belongs to his real I.

Left to himself a man has only fleeting glimpses of this situation, brief flashes of truth which he forgets or covers up and whose meaning he is not able to grasp. He does not see that in spite of what he believes in his waking state, his lower being is not completed. His physical organism alone has reached maturity, and with it a personality has developed to the limit of its growth. Both have come to the end of their natural development, which is much more external than inner, and beyond which nature, having no need for man to progress further, has provided nothing else for him.

In order for further development to take place, he must awake to possibilities of another order: the development of his real I, that is, of his inner being.

However, this kind of awakening and the development of these possibilities do not come about of themselves; they require great efforts intentionally directed toward that aim. A man's individuality, his real "I," can only start to grow from his essence: it could be said that the individuality of a man is his essence fully grown up.

Just as awakening does not take place by itself, so there are always new obstacles in the way of growth; and the obstacles to the growth of essence are contained in personality. In order for this growth to take place very definite conditions are necessary: precise efforts by the man himself and appropriate help from those who have gone before him on the way of development. This amounts to saying that the only place where such growth is possible is in a school where a man can work on the awakening and development of his real I.

Failing these conditions, if a man is left to himself and to his own initiative, little by little the flashes of truth die out and the glimmers of true consciousness fade away. His personality takes up all the room. All hope of individual evolution is finally lost for him. In spite of possibilities of another order, he is, and will have been, only a specimen of higher animality; and having served the ends of great nature, all that is left for him is to "die like a dog." Ordinary man, man the machine, is only dust and to dust he returns.

The third state of consciousness is the state of "self-consciousness," or consciousness of one's own being, developed precisely through this awakening to one's self.

It is usually taken for granted that we possess this state of consciousness or that we can have it at will together with all the qualities related to it: inner unity, a permanent I, will, freedom, and so on.

Actually, observation shows us that we do not possess this state, and that our wish for it, however strong, is incapable of creating it in ourselves. We have only faint glimpses of it with no means of interpreting them correctly. And we have no theoretical information about this state (or almost none), precisely because men imagine they already have it, so in general they have considered the study of it pointless.

In fact this third state of consciousness is a natural right of man as he is, and if he does not possess it, it is solely on account of the abnormal conditions in which he lives.

This state is the result of "growth"—one might also call it a gradual revelation—and it is impossible to make it more or less permanent without long work and a special training connected with the functioning in man of the higher emotional center, as well as the establishment of right relations between this center, the lower centers, and their functions.

This state is connected with the development of a support, which is called the second body (different traditional teachings give it different names). This body serves as a support for the perceptions and manifestations peculiar to this level of life, as well as for the functions which are characteristic of it, of which the most important one is an authentic "feeling of myself."

Three qualities also belong to this state: permanent self-consciousness, free attention and independent will. From all three together there results a permanent presence to oneself which confers on man in this state an individuality which he did not possess until then and a personal sense of responsibility which he could not have had as long as his individuality had not been realized.

But everything that can be said about such a state remains somewhat hypothetical for us. In our waking state, we have only two ways of approaching it, two kinds of special moments which life sometimes brings and whose value we generally sense without understanding very well why. The first are those glimmers of consciousness of what we are which are given us in serious moments of emergency—at a moment when one's life is in danger, for example, or at the loss of a loved one—which make a very deep impression on us. The second are moments of inner awareness, of a conscience which is our own, which we find intuitively when life puts everything in question for us and which forces us to look deeply within ourselves and respond "to the very best of our knowledge and belief" and no longer on behalf of an acquired morality and ready-made ideas.

Such moments are the approach to a state of "objective conscience"—the same for everyone who has reached the state of self-consciousness—in which a man feels in an immediate and total way everything it is possible for him to feel.

Conscience of this kind brings serenity to one who has attained inner unity and who has got rid of inner contradictions. It brings suffering to one in whom such contradictions still exist. Brought to light by conscience, they become generators of "objective remorse of conscience." This would be an unbearable experience if given suddenly to an ordinary man who is altogether made up of contradictions. But there are psychological mechanisms which cover it up and form "buffers." It is only rarely that a man finds an intuitive approach to it in certain special moments when he feels called to his own inner conscience, which exists independently of acquired ideas.

For a man who has tasted the possibility of being himself, the only chance is to seek out and find a school where he can work toward rediscovering his real I, the reality of which he has glimpsed in special moments.

Paradoxically we have much more theoretical information on the fourth state attainable by man, objective consciousness. This is so even though we have no experience of it whatever, and, such as we are, cannot possibly attain it without long work, and without passing through the third state, that of self-consciousness.

This is actually the state very many people aspire to, knowing deeply in themselves that they do not have it. The search for the "great virtues," for universal love, for the triumph of justice, freedom, objectivity, and many other things—as well as for the "ideal"—is fundamentally motivated by the presentiment, the intuition, rooted in us, that such a state exists.

We know nothing about it, and the only approach available to us is no doubt what can be called an "intellectual intuition," which is given us at certain moments and which is, as it were, "instinctive," just as the impulse of "conscience" represents for us the instinctive approach to the third state. For ordinary man, this is an experience in which one senses in oneself immediately and completely how little one knows, how many contradictions there are in what one knows, and what is the direction of the movement toward "Truth." In a completely realized man, this experience unites with the objective Great Knowledge, characteristic of the fourth state.

We can have no idea at all of what this state actually is. We may know that it is connected with the functioning of the higher intellectual center and with the growth of a third body, the spiritual body. We may know that it includes a state of universal presence, objective Knowledge, and a feeling of universal being—and the powers for their manifestation, a level of consciousness, attention and creative will—of which an ordinary man can have no conception.

Only one who has reached the state of self-consciousness can have flashes of the state of objective consciousness and be able to remember them. An ordinary man, brought by artificial means into this state, remembers nothing when he returns to his usual state, and thinks only that he "lost consciousness" for a time.

However, this state is the state which many people would like to reach directly, without passing through the state of self-consciousness (believing that they already possess it, or that it is as illusory as the ordinary state), and certain ascetic disciplines have been developed for this purpose. Even granting that some people may have reached it, and this is possible "artificially," such a realization nevertheless represents a dead end, which, because one of the levels of his being is missing, makes impossible for a man the ultimate achievement of transcending all individuality and, above all, makes impossible his return to ordinary life without losing the full reality which self-realization brings to it.

Actually, there exists another, supreme "state," which is beyond those we have already spoken of and which cannot even be called a state.

The four states of presence possible for man in his life are individual states, however vast and formless they may be. This last state is the supreme Realization (the Buddhist *paranirvana,* the cosmic mind of Zen, the *Yahweh* in the Kabbalah, the unconditioned Absolute of metaphysics—beyond all form and all individuality).

It is "That" which cannot be named, about which nothing can be said, about which nothing can be known, which can only be spoken about in terms of what it is not, and which is also referred to by such terms as "annihilation," "extinction," "fullness of the Void," "formlessness." But it is not nothingness, nor shadow, nor light, nor emptiness, nor fullness; for there all distinctions and differences cease to exist.

This is the ultimate end, where a man dissolves in the supreme Realization.

Centers and functions

If we intend to study ourselves and know ourselves, we must proceed just as we would in the study of any other complex machine: we must know the various parts, the way they mesh with each other, the energy they use, and how the energy sets the machine in motion. We also need to know the conditions in which the machine works correctly and what causes it to work wrongly.

Foremost among the parts of our machine are the being centers, or brains, and the functions which express them in life.

According to the way of envisaging man's structure that we have adopted as being the most realistic and the most useful for our study, the complete human machine consists of seven such formations. Four of them take care of its everyday functioning, our basic participation in life; the other three, over and above this, are more specifically the support for the individuality in the proper sense of the word.

The four ordinary formations which take care of our everyday life include:

1. the intellectual, with the function of ideation and thought;

2. the emotional, with the function of emotions and feelings;

3. the moving, with the function of movement in space and all the outer work of the organism;

4. the instinctive, with the function of automatic maintenance of the organic life of the organism and all its internal work.

A fifth formation plays a part, on the one hand, in our ordinary life (this is the only aspect of it which is usually recognized), and on the other, in the development of true individuality. This is the sexual formation, a function of the masculine or feminine principle in all its manifestations, the outcome of which is participation in "creation," that is, creation at the level at which sex is functioning.

Over and above these, there are in man two more formations, from which he is almost entirely cut off. Ordinary man is not aware of their existence. They appear only in higher states of presence, and ordinary language has no words for them. Knowledge of them is confined to "schools":

—one is the higher emotional center (with its function), which is connected with the state of being present to oneself. When a higher and permanent I is present, forming a stable individuality endowed with the corresponding faculties of self-consciousness, attention and will, then real feelings appear—that is, a true feeling of self and feelings of a higher order that are linked with it.

—the other is the higher intellectual center (with its function), which is expressed in objective thinking. It is connected with a state of universal being and presence, endowed with objective consciousness and with being feelings which ordinary man scarcely knows.

Ordinary man, in fact, does not "possess" these states of higher consciousness, and we cannot truly study them or experience them. We know of their existence only indirectly from those who have attained them. In our ordinary state we only have glimmers of self-consciousness in certain circumstances: these are lightning flashes of contact with our higher emotional center; but without special work we do not understand what they mean.

Deeply buried in us and usually stifled by the development of personality, there lies an intuitive approach to what these two states might be; the first state appears in the form of impulses of "conscience," and the second as what might be called "intellectual intuition."

There are many studies of or allusions to these higher states of consciousness and the higher functions which go with them in religions and philosophical doctrines and writings. These allusions are all the more difficult for us to understand because we do not know how to differentiate between the two states. What we hear spoken of as ecstasy, *samadhi*, cosmic consciousness, illumination, and so on, may refer either to one state or the other—sometimes to experiences of self-consciousness and sometimes to experiences of objective consciousness. Paradoxically, it is about the highest state, objective consciousness, from which we are totally cut off, that we are generally given more information. This is in part because we imagine we already know and possess the intermediate state of self-consciousness. Although the state of objective consciousness can only be attained through and after that of self-consciousness, we are almost never interested in the latter. And so, no evolution is possible for us: intellectual and rational development, however broad, cannot by themselves lead to the state of objective consciousness or to the Great Knowledge. The normal evolution of man is possible only by passing through the state of self-consciousness.

The first four functions are sufficient for our ordinary life, and this is spent in one or another of three states of presence, each having a characteristic level of consciousness by which it is usually distinguished from the others. These are the three levels of life given to us naturally—sleep, the waking state, and flashes of self-consciousness (which actually cannot yet be rightly spoken of as a state).

Each of our four functions can be manifested in each of these three states, but in quite different ways. In our sleep, their manifestations are disjointed, with no apparent basis.

They act automatically and almost completely escape us; at the very most we can only get bits and pieces of information about ourselves from them, and in any case it is impossible to make the functions serve useful purposes.

In our state of waking consciousness, which is a state of relative consciousness, where a more or less coherent link is established between the mind and each of the other functions, we already have a certain control over them; their functioning can be watched, their results can be compared, verified, straightened out to some extent, and although they may fabricate many illusions they can give us some sense of direction. They are all we have, and we have no choice but to make what we can of them. If, however, we knew how many incomplete and illusory observations, erroneous theories, wrong deductions and false conclusions these functions bring us, we would altogether stop believing in what they tell us and in what they make out of us. But as we are, we cannot see how deceptive these observations, beliefs, and theories are. We continue to believe in them and in "ourselves."

This is just what prevents us from fully appreciating the rare moments of the third state of consciousness, the state of self-consciousness, when for a brief instant it takes over control of our functions, usually leaving us with an unforgettable impression of life.

All this means that consciousness and the functions are closely related to states of presence; nevertheless, they are different parts of our machine. Our various functions can be manifested at every moment, and the quality both of their manifestations and of their reciprocal relationships changes according to the states or levels of presence at which they are functioning. At the furthest extremes, functions can exist without presence, and presence can exist without functions. Examples of the former situation can be found in ourselves right now, by honest observation. As to the second situation, we can know nothing about it so long as we have not already developed a strong enough state of presence in ourselves.

As a matter of fact, the functions are the expression in life of the centers, their manifestation; taken all together they give each human being his own particular character. The functions are more accessible to us than the centers, so self-study must begin with them: they are our way of responding to life, and therefore we can observe them.

The centers, on the other hand, are much more hidden, placed at the very core of our being. They pertain to our essence, and their particular features characterize our individuality in the proper sense of the term, but nothing is more difficult to see. In fact, they belong to the realm of the unconscious.

Each center, in reality, pervades the whole body, penetrating as it were our entire organism. At the same time, each center possesses its own center of gravity, or brain, which forms in us a distinct and independent "being-localization." These localizations manage the potential of the vital energy, undifferentiated at first, which is made available to each being at birth or assimilated by him during his growth and life.

The number of centers is the same as the number of functions which express them, namely, in the case of man, seven. But for preliminary study, the centers are much less accessible than our functions. Not only do we remain cut off from our two higher centers, of which we can have no direct knowledge, but also we know hardly anything of the sex center except the organic level of its functioning.

Lastly, in ordinary man, the instinctive and moving centers (which take care of the inner and outer work of the machine) are closely connected, and, in addition, are closely related to the organic part of the sex center, forming with it a functionally balanced whole. Thus it is not too great an approximation, and does not falsify man's nature, to consider him as a being who functions in three ways—organically, emotionally and intellectually—and who is endowed with three brains functioning at three different levels in himself.

This three-brained structure, as opposed to that of two-brained or one-brained beings, is what offers each man the possibility of relating to the three fundamental creative forces of the universe, and, hence, the possibility of autonomous evolution.

We may go on to ask ourselves what these "independent being-localizations," or brains, are. Actually, they are not functionally independent, because, being interconnected, anything which affects one of them also has an effect on the other two.

The brain which serves as the principal support for the transformations (reception, concentration and realization) of the first fundamental force (the affirmative, positive, or active force) is at the intellectual level, and is located in the head.

The brain which serves as the principal support for the transformations of the second fundamental force (the negative, receptive, or passive force) is at the organic level, and is located in the spinal column, or, more exactly, the cerebrospinal axis.

As for the brain which serves as the principal support for the transformations of the third fundamental force (the reconciling or neutralizing force or the force of relationship), it is divided into a number of parts whose localizations vary according to their specific functioning, but which are so closely interrelated that they function as one whole. The most important of these parts form the solar plexus, and taken all together they correspond roughly to what is known as the sympathetic nervous system or the neuro-hormonal system, upon which the affective or emotional state of man depends.

The primordial life energy, entering man through his foods, separates in him, for purposes of assimilation, into its three basic constituents—active, negative and reconciling. If the conditions of man's life were normal, these constituents would be distributed among the three levels which correspond to them, namely, the organic, higher emotional and higher intellectual, in order to realize in him the three sources for a fully developed entity.

But as a result of the abnormal conditions of his life and, in particular, the absence of direct interconnections between the centers, as well as the absence of a connection between the organic level and the higher centers, ordinary man today lives almost exclusively on the organic level, with only a remote reflection of what his true emotional and intellectual life could be. Because man lacks a real and all-inclusive presence, only his organic part, namely, his planetary body (with its physical, emotional and mental levels) is able to receive, both for itself and for its participation in the development of an individuality, the share of life energy to which it is entitled. This is assimilated by the moving center, the instinctive center, and the lower level of the sex center. The remainder of the energy, corresponding principally to the affirming force and the reconciling force, is lost to man so long as he does not produce a special effort of presence which would permit him, to a greater or lesser degree, to receive and assimilate it for beginning the elaboration of the two higher bodies without which his individuality can never attain its full development. (This is connected with the "alchemy" of the first and second conscious shocks that Gurdjieff explains in detail in his book and in the "food diagram" of Ouspensky's book.)

The life of ordinary man today, maintained by his four lower centers and functions, remains within a purely planetary order and offers no hope of leading him beyond it. Man is still in fact no more than a higher animal so long as his possibilities of another order remain undeveloped. The only thing that distinguishes him from an animal is the existence of these possibilities in him—but only insofar as delay in their development has not yet caused them to atrophy.

The centers use an energy that derives, more or less indirectly, from the universal life force, and which corresponds to the quality of the "substance" of which they are made or, one might even say, to their frequency of vibration.

But the centers are not connected directly to this source of energy: it is brought to them with the different kinds of "food," or elements which enter the organism. These entering elements, differing in materiality and quality, cannot be used directly, but they can be absorbed, thanks to a work of assimilation peculiar to each of them, and thus participate in the individual for the maintenance and construction of the corresponding "substance"; the rest passes through the organism unhindered and thus is eliminated. According to the ideas given by Gurdjieff, these "foods" are of three kinds: the ordinary food we are quite familiar with, the atmosphere we breathe (of which air is only the most concrete element), and the impressions we receive. As for the parts of these elements that correspond to the natural level of man's development, their assimilation takes place automatically by means of the mechanisms which make up the organism; but an altogether different part of these same elements becomes assimilable when the support of the corresponding "substances," together with appropriate modes of "nutrition," have been developed by work on oneself.

Such ideas, when we first hear them, may strike us as fantastic. However, if we are attentive to them, we may recognize that we have in ourselves intimations which should be enough to prompt us toward a deeper study of the sources of our vital energy and the conditions for refining the qualities of our life. Thus we are well aware that a coarse and heavy diet does not tend to improve the quality of our work or the subtlety of our psychic perceptions. We also know that the environment in which we live and the degree of refinement of our social circle are important factors in the development in ourselves of the corresponding qualities of understanding. Finally the human relationships we establish and the influences we either accept or refuse have an important place in determining the possibilities of our inner evolution. The study of the conditions in which the various foods can be received and assimilated is thus a "vital" necessity for every man who wishes to work for his own transformation; it is one of the conditions of his evolution.

But the specific amount of energy available to each of the centers at a given moment, for example to carry out a task required of it, is not unlimited; it is only the reserve which it has managed to accumulate. Gurdjieff, recorded by Ouspensky, gives an arresting picture of this reservoir of energy and the manner in which it can be used.[1] According to this description everything takes place as if there existed in the human machine, alongside each center, two small accumulators for the specific functional energy that it uses. These small accumulators are connected with each other and with the corresponding center. There also exists in the organism a large accumulator of vital energy (connected with being) with which each pair of small accumulators is linked up. This large accumulator is in a sense the central reserve of undifferentiated energy, which (provided that it is itself correctly fed) it separates according to need into energies appropriate for each center.

1. Cf. Ouspensky, *In Search of the Miraculous*, pp. 233-236 (from which the essentials of this description are extracted).

When a center is working—whether the intellectual, emotional, moving or instinctive center—it draws the energy it needs from one of the two small accumulators. If this work goes on long enough, the energy in that accumulator is finally used up; the work slows down and then becomes impossible. At that moment a break, a brief rest, sometimes a shock from outside, or a further effort, makes possible a connection with the second small accumulator; the work starts up again with new energy and fresh possibilities, while in the meantime the first accumulator recharges. If the work continues on, the second accumulator in turn becomes exhausted: another pause, another outer shock, and the connection with the first accumulator is re-established.

Everything therefore depends on the intensity of the work and the tempo of the expenditure of energy. If this is rightly measured out and is adapted to the tempo of the recharging by the central accumulator, the work begins again with the same possibilities as before. If, for one reason or another, the quantity and tempo of the expenditure exceeds that of the recharging, the new connection is made before the recharging is finished and the supply of energy is exhausted more rapidly. One depletion follows another, and in the end neither accumulator has any more energy to give and the work cannot continue. The man feels really tired, and normally the work has to stop.

However, in a case of pressing necessity and provided the importance of the work is deeply felt, a man can go beyond even this fatigue and find a new supply of energy, through the center being directly connected to the large accumulator. The large accumulator contains an enormous amount of energy, and when a man is connected to it he can make apparently superhuman efforts. However, if the demand for energy is too great, that is, if the expenditure is faster and bigger than the recharge brought in by food, air and impressions, the large accumulator itself runs out and the organism dies.

But this happens only as an exception: for an organism to die of exhaustion would require special conditions. Long before real danger of that, the organism reacts and by various means stops functioning: the man faints, falls asleep, or develops some illness that forces him to stop.

The small accumulators do not have a very large reserve of energy. They have enough for daily needs and the ordinary requirements of life. But for any important undertaking, and especially for the work on oneself, for inner growth and for the efforts required of everyone who commits himself to a way of evolution, the energy of the small accumulators is not enough. A man who commits himself to this kind of search, therefore, has to learn to draw energy directly from the big accumulator, and to establish, whenever needed, a direct connection between this accumulator and one or another of his centers; so long as he is unable to do this, he fails in these undertakings and "goes to sleep" before his efforts can yield the least result.

Results are possible only with the help of the emotional center. The emotional center is much more subtle than the three others (especially if one takes into account that the intellectual center ordinarily works only with its lower part, the formatory apparatus) and, by its very nature, is much better fitted for making this direct connection. It is in situations where the emotional center is violently involved that one sees this connection occur most often, and one can learn to make it intentionally. It is through the emotional center that a man can succeed in mobilizing the energy needed for his further evolution and become able to take upon himself the necessary super-efforts, including those which clear the way for the development of the higher parts of his intellectual center, which cannot be done by the intellectual center alone.

Thus the centers and their functions make up a complex

combination that is very important to know. They are at the same time receivers of energy, recorders, transformers (or rather, selectors) and transmitters.

Each center is an apparatus for receiving energy and works to take in the various elements that are the three kinds of food for the machine. But to be able to blend with the energy potential of the organism, these foods must be adapted in such a way that they can be assimilated by the large accumulator, from which each center will then draw the quality of energy proper to it. The centers themselves cannot take their food directly. This taking in of energy by the human machine, and the way in which these energies can be made digestible, gives us a glimpse of a complex inner alchemy, which, to be understood, requires special and difficult study. For example, some impressions or influences taken in by the centers, such as planetary influences, come from far away or from somewhere not apparent to us. On the other hand, in the organism, each kind of food goes through special transformations by which some of its constituent parts are assimilated and others rejected. Furthermore, each transformation of energy has its particular circuits.

Each center is also a selector and, to some degree, a transformer. The center draws from the central reservoir (where energy accumulates in forms that depend on the level of the evolution of the being) the energy corresponding to its "essential" nature and its level of functioning, and in each individual gives the energy the characteristics inherent in his own structure, that is to say, corresponding to the characteristics of his essence.

Each center is also a transmitting apparatus by virtue of the functions required of it which it is called on to perform in the inner or outer life of the individual.

Finally, each center has its own memory. Attached to its

transmitting-receiving part there are recording apparatuses made of sensitive matter, which would be compared today to computer memory banks, but which Gurdjieff likened to blank cylinders of wax. Everything that happens to us, all that we see, hear, do and learn, is recorded on these rolls. Every inner and outer event leaves an impression on these rolls. It is indeed a matter of impressions, imprints which may be deep or superficial and which may also be fleeting and disappear very quickly without leaving a trace. Moreover, these inscriptions or impressions engraved on the rolls of the different centers are linked together at the level of the ordinary mind by associations.

These associations are very important for understanding the functioning of the machine. The machine is so constructed that, in certain conditions, the recording of impressions on the rolls automatically creates a tendency for some of them to connect together, so that when one is evoked all those associated with it are recalled. Such associations are produced chiefly in two sets of circumstances: first, when impressions received together by one or several centers are inscribed simultaneously on corresponding rolls; and second, when impressions engraved on the same roll or on rolls of different centers have a certain similarity (so that they are mutually aroused by a phenomenon analogous to resonance).

These two automatic processes of association need to be known by any man who wishes to have his machine serve his own evolution. The first in particular can very quickly be made use of. Indeed, for a moment different impressions received simultaneously on one or several rolls are by this very fact linked together; not only do they remain in the memory longer than isolated impressions, but also the recollection of one inevitably causes the others to be remembered at the same time. If a man comes to realize, at least for a moment, a degree of unity in himself, all the impressions received together on such an occasion by the different centers become linked and remain linked in his memory, thus helping to establish this unity.

But the second process is just as important. Impressions having a certain inner similarity are also evoked by one another and leave a deeper trace; this relationship is automatically established when similar impressions are repeated in the same center. This is the basis of the conditioning and habits which maintain the mechanicalness of ordinary life. But if a man, through special work, becomes more conscious, then more subtle and more complete relationships of inherent similarity are established between his different rolls, and put at his disposal an aggregate in which all the life impressions are associated together at the different levels.

As opposed to this, in a state of identification where a man is absorbed in outer functionings, he does not even notice the events which may be impressing his centers, or, if he does notice them, their traces are deposited in him unconsciously and disappear before they have been evaluated or associated, thus leaving no trace at all in his memory.

Each center taken separately, and the individual with his centers taken as a whole, has therefore a passive side and is a receiver more or less open to the energies that reach it; and it also has an active side, which more or less effectively influences the forms of his life; and, between these two, it has a selective action responsible for the particular quality it confers on this utilization of its energy.

Among all these notions which may at first seem to us rather arbitrary, the clearest for us is that each center has its own specific characteristics. It is important to know these characteristics if one is in search of self-knowledge—this is one of the first aims in self-observation. At present, we can know little or nothing about the parts of ourselves from which we are habitually cut off (the two higher functions, and the higher levels of the sex function). But we can observe the four functions with which we ordinarily live. The idea is that by repeatedly observing these functions, it becomes possible for us little by little to be aware of the characteristic features of each of them at their source, that is, in the moment the function arises from the center as an original impulse, and thereby we may perhaps arrive at knowledge of these centers, that is, a knowledge of our own essence, without which there is no self-knowledge. But this is not possible at the beginning, and to avoid the risk of serious mistakes observation of ourselves can only begin by observing our four primary functions: intellectual, emotional, moving and instinctive. This observation comprises two stages, two levels: these functions must at first be observed and recognized in all their outer manifestations; later, it becomes possible to observe them within oneself, through struggling to recognize and understand the fundamental inner tendencies which give them the outer form in which we manifest.

The difficulty of this kind of observation is immediately apparent: in fact, not only do we have many functions, always mixed up with each other in each situation, with one of them predominating to some degree, but also, due to our ignorance, we constantly confuse them with each other. This confusion is all the greater in that different functions may look very much alike and the same manifestations may come from different sources in us. Our observations are also complicated by the fact that our functions look very different according to the state in which we happen to be, which is constantly changing. So we have to begin by observing simple situations in which a single, easily recognizable function is clearly dominant, allowing us to experience directly its source in ourselves. Eventually, with experience, it becomes easier to recognize in oneself the interplay of the functions and even to have, in a given moment of presence, true flashes of self-remembering.

Thought is the function of the intellectual center. All mental processes are included in this: the reception of intellectual data, analysis, comparison, the formation of ideas, and of reasoning and imagining, and recording in the intellectual memory.

But thought is of various kinds (and qualities), according to the level on which this center is working. As we shall see, self-observation leads us to the conclusion that the ideas which are our ordinary mode of thought are of a purely mechanical order. Because of their automatic arising in the face of every impression that impinges on the mind, their unceasing flow, their continual associations, their comparisons and systematically reactive responses, they make up in us what can be called the "formatory" apparatus or mind (sometimes wrongly called the formatory "center," for it is not a center but only a switchboard), with which we habitually respond to almost all life situations. Even what we call "reflection" is left to it more often than not.

This way of looking at the "thought" by which we ordinarily live, and with which almost all of what man has accomplished has been done, is obviously hard to accept at first and becomes acceptable only when another form of thought has been experienced.

Indeed, for the intellectual center to become capable of other than purely reactive and automatic thinking, it has to function on another level, the level of a presence and of a stable, all-enveloping, soundly established I. Then independent thoughts are possible with a development, true "reflection," and foresight that conform with our overall sense of individuality and which characterize real "subjective" thought.

As for a third level of thought which is held out as a possibility and which would be real "objective" thought, ordinary man has no knowledge of it. It is on a still higher level, and pertains to the higher intellectual center.

At all levels, the function of the intellect is affirmation and negation: yes or no. The intellect receives the data, compares them with what it knows, coordinates, conceptualizes and looks ahead. On the lowest level, it is automatic critical judgment and imagination; on a higher level, it is logical confrontation and foresight. As for objective thought, we can know nothing about it, but we may suppose that it conforms with the Great Knowledge and that its power of foreknowledge is in conformity with the universal laws that govern the world and everything in it, as well as with the original cause of these laws. This may call up in us an analogy with the Logos, or the Word of Genesis, but we must certainly recognize that with our ordinary thought we are not really able to grasp such ideas.

Feeling is the function of the emotional center. All the emotional processes are included—joy, sorrow, grief, fear, surprise, and so on—but observation soon shows us that we are often unable to recognize them and are constantly confusing them with the functionings of other centers. In particular, one important difficulty arises from the fact that instinctive shocks, which only concern the life of the organic body (for example, certain fears) are felt by us in a manner very similar to emotional shocks, and thus are very often taken for emotions.

The emotional center "experiences": each time that an impression reaches it, it likes or dislikes, and experiences a personal approval or disapproval of the impression that is manifested in the form of an emotion. Because of this, each time something touches the person and his emotional functioning, it is automatically accepted or rejected, and at the same time a positive or negative emotion is expressed. This "something" is felt as desirable or undesirable. But these operations of the emotional center depend entirely on the level of presence; in man's ordinary state, only one of his personages is there and so it is only a matter of emotions (partial feelings inherent in one single aspect of oneself) and not of real feeling (all-inclusive feeling inherent in the total presence of a really established inner I). Man in his ordinary state has no true feeling. He has only automatic emotions, the emotions of reaction, depending entirely on which personage is present. The personage changes according to circumstances, and its "feeling" changes with it; but man does not see these changes and, in his emotional part more than in any other, believes himself to be endowed with a permanence and a continuity which he does not have.

The emotional center becomes capable of real feeling only when a stable presence, relatively independent of the surrounding circumstances, has been developed. This presence is built up around a feeling of self which animates it and gives to its life at every moment a sense of being what it is. Schematically, we may say that emotions belong to personality and feelings to the real being—I. The feeling of self which accompanies awakening to oneself is the first real feeling that a man can have; further evolution of the emotional center, going hand in hand with the attainment of a real I, approaches progressively the level of refinement of the higher emotional center, makes contact with it and finally merges with it. Not until this level is reached do the great "objective" feelings of Faith, Hope and Love become possible for man.

On all levels, the function of feeling is valuation and personal relationship; on all levels, the emotional center experiences, values, and to one degree or another consents. True feelings are not negative: they have no negative aspect.

A true feeling can be more intense or less, greater or smaller; otherwise it does not exist, and is merely indifference—the higher emotional center has no negativity. At the ordinary level, on the contrary, on the plane of the emotions, the emotional center agrees or refuses and the emotions which we live with can be positive, neutral or negative according to how they strike the emotionality—that is to say the specific self-love—which animates each of our personages.

Movement is the function of the moving center. It includes all such outer movements as walking, writing, speaking, eating, and so on. The function of the moving center is thus movement or rest, action or inaction, and a deeper or more superficial degree of relaxation. We perceive our form and the degree of its activity through sensation. The physical sensation of himself allows a man at any moment to know what his attitude is and what his activity is, and eventually to have control over them; hence its fundamental importance in the search for self-knowledge.

The characteristic of the moving center is its passivity. It has no initiative of its own, and by nature it remains inert, but it obeys at once whatever is there to call upon it to serve. This explains why it is often difficult, especially at the lower levels of activity of the machine, to distinguish between what belongs to the moving center and what comes from the part that is making use of it. It does not lean on any one center in particular. Like the other centers (as we shall see later) it has its own thinking (the intelligence of movement), its own instinct, its own emotionality, and the possibility of an activity of its own which, because of its extreme passivity, is only realized in exceptional circumstances. Again, because of its passivity, one of the moving center's chief characteristics is its capacity for imitation. The moving center imitates what it sees without reasoning; it is able to conform absolutely to a model and to reproduce the model's behavior exactly without changing anything. Even for apparently rather complex behavior such imitation is still arrived at through engagement of the moving center alone; however, beyond a certain level of complexity, the other centers in turn become involved, at least at the related motor level.

Another characteristic of the moving center is that all of its behavior has to be learned. The motor functions in man, as well as those of animals, have to be learned, and the moving center is generally endowed with a remarkable memory. This is what makes it possible to differentiate between moving functions and instinctive functions, which are innate. Man has very few outer movements which are innate; animals have more in varying degrees according to the species. But what is usually called "instinct" in animals is in fact more often a collection of complex motor habits which young animals learn from older ones by imitation.

Observation of the way the moving center functions in oneself very soon brings out an important idea: the normal functioning of the moving center (similar to the functioning of the instinctive center but contrary to that of the emotional and intellectual centers whose level depends on the degree of presence) is a relatively independent functioning. The moving center is capable by itself, within the limits that are possible for it, of carrying out the work required of it without any direct intervention by the part which requires it, except a simple preliminary training, thereafter needing no control beyond "supervision" (surveillance and adaptation) of the work carried out and the result obtained. And the moving center normally works in this way both in ordinary life and on the higher levels of life. However, in ordinary life, due to what we shall see is the wrong work of centers, there are many anomalies—abnormal relationships, contradictory instructions and pointless interruptions, not to speak of the natural laziness of the moving center, come in, constantly disorganize its work, and put themselves in its place falsely. So long as a stable and thoroughly coherent presence has not been established, and is not there to direct it, the work of the moving center cannot be effective in ordinary conditions or participate in a real "doing," an authentic act. In ordinary man, the moving center, even though given a good training for daily life, sometimes serves a variety of interests. It suffers from incessant changes, rivalries, intrusions and stoppages. Arising from all this, its actions, since they are based on blind habits, end up by having no continuity, and in the immediate present are often a "failure." The worst of it is that a man who acts in this way has later to suffer the consequences of his carelessness. An unfortunate action done unconsciously may quite often (but not always) be made good later at the cost of a new conscious effort of work (undertaken either by the one who acted or another), although a much harder one than would have been needed for the correct action. But every action does produce consequences and in no case can the results of an action be wiped out. The law that links causes to effects, particularly perceptible on the moving level, is inescapable, and man bears inescapably the burden of his actions, conscious or otherwise.

The function of the instinctive center is control of the inner life of the organism, and its perceptions are expressed through satisfaction or need. It is the center of "instinctive" attractions and repulsions, the center of organic impressions of "good" or "bad" which regulate the life of the machine and which taken all together make for organic well-being or discomfort, and even pain.

Because this function operates in the dark within us and only emerges into our ordinary consciousness in moments of excess, a great deal of confusion arises in regard to it, and it is customary to call instinctive many things which are not. This expression can only be applied to the internal functions of the organism: breathing, circulation, digestion, neuro-sensory perception, the function of movement and all the internal functions such as the production of heat, assimilation, hormonal stimulation, the growth and maintenance of forms, with all their inner regulation, including certain reflexes. Our instinctive functions form an entire inner world. What is characteristic of them, and makes them recognizable, is that they are innate. Many other actions, which are not innate but acquired, likewise take place in us in the dark without our being aware of them—all of them are automatisms. They may belong to any one of the centers: thus there is automatic thinking (our ideas), automatic feeling (our emotions), and, in a more general sense, an automatic—that is to say totally unconscious—part in each center: there is an entire automatic life in us which may interfere at certain points with our instinctive life, but is completely different.

Knowledge and control of this instinctive life is possible; to a certain extent, it always goes together with self-knowledge. A deepening of this knowledge and the mastery of it are possible by means of special exercises, which are difficult and dangerous, but are followed in certain disciplines and may be part of a way of evolution. But beyond a certain level—indispensible for the harmonious functioning of the organism—such mastery is not necessary for the development of the higher parts of the human being.

As for the sex function, it is the one, due to the structure of the sex center, which uses the finest energy and serves the highest function of the organism, namely, participation in the work of creation at the corresponding level. It could be said of the sex center that it is the center of the gift of oneself.

It gives a coloring of its own polarity, masculine or feminine (reflecting on the human plane the two fundamental forces, active and receptive), to the entire life of each one of us. Depending on the polarity, the vital force gives or is given. However, this polarity is only relative; it depends upon the level in relation to which it is being considered, and any force on a given level (this is a general law) is receptive in relation to the level above and active in relation to the level below it.

Some modern schools of psychology, especially the original branches of psychoanalysis, which are questionable on many points, sought to explain the whole development and behavior of the human being on the basis of the sex function, taking it as the prime mover, evolutionary axis and chief motivation of the life of every human being. This rather narrow point of view has fortunately broadened in the course of time and the idea of the "libido" has been extended to stand for the "wish to be" in general. It is obvious that, as soon as it comes into play, the sex center, thanks to the fine quality of the energy it uses, brings much more subtlety, acuity and speed to sensory perceptions, impressions and the functions. It is also clear that sexual fulfillment leading to the reproduction of life is the crowning achievement of all the organic activity of the human being, and without this fulfillment all of this activity, from the organic and natural point of view, is so to speak cut short. But this does not exclude the possibility, from the point of view of higher development of the human being, that this same sexual energy, the finest and most active of the energies which are available to man, should serve not for the reproduction of organic life but for the realization of a higher order of life (a new birth, the opening up of another level of life) which can only come about starting from energy of this quality, from whatever there is of "creative" energy in man. In this context, a certain number of traditional schools or ways demand that their disciples abstain from the use of sexual energy on the organic level. Those who do not take sides on this difficult question realize that no such absolute attitude can be the answer; for, here again, everything is relative and depends on each particular being and at the same time on the stage of his evolution. Only a certain amount of sex energy can be transformed at any given time to serve the development of a higher level of being; if some of this energy is left over (and this depends on each individual's particular functioning), this excess has to be used up in the natural way because its accumulation results in abnormal usages and irregular intrusions of this energy in the other functions of the machine (in the form of bad work of the centers, even to the point of perversion). If allowed to become established as automatic habits of the mechanism, these irregular usages of sex energy may become predominant and monopolize it so much that all hope of a man's evolution to a higher level becomes impossible.

In fact, in ordinary man, the sex center almost never works with its own energy, autonomously. It nearly always depends on one of the other centers—the intellectual, the emotional, the moving or instinctive—which for its purpose of coming to a higher quality makes use of the specifically sexual energy. Perhaps this is what has so much influenced certain aspects of psychoanalytic theory, which, incidentally, was first worked out from observations derived from the study of hypnotic or trance states based on pathological cases. This habitual dependence of the sex function can be explained mostly by the fact that the sex function in man, although present from birth, only develops comparatively late in life, after the other four functions are already more or less well developed. (It is not the same way with animals.) The sex center certainly does exist from the time of birth, manifesting intermittently and unconsciously in the automatism. But its real development and function appear only after the almost complete evolution of the other parts, and so are largely conditioned by them. The result is that no real study of the sex center can be profitably undertaken until the other functions in all their manifestations are known completely.

Another difference between the sex center and the other lower centers is that it is not, in reality, limited to their level alone, but gives a color to the whole human individual, whatever degree of evolution has been reached, so long as any trace of individuality remains. But ordinary man lives only at the lower, organic level of his sex center. At this level, the instinctive, moving and sex centers form a balanced unit, working on the same plane and able to receive the corresponding impulses of the three fundamental forces. Thus the organic life of the machine is able to continue indefinitely on its own. The sex center plays the neutralizing role here in relation to the moving and instinctive centers; sometimes one and sometimes the other of these is active or passive, according to states and circumstances.

The structure itself of the centers is worth looking at in detail; as we make use only of scattered fragments of them, it is difficult for us to see this structure and to have a view of it as a whole.

An outstanding characteristic of the four lower centers of the human machine is that they can be receptive to the positive side or the negative side of every impression that reaches them. The right functioning of the centers, as regards which aspect they take from the impressions they receive, is extremely important, because these two aspects of everything, positive and negative, are necessary for right orientation in life. More often than not (depending on the characteristics of the individual essence) the centers are naturally more receptive to one of the aspects than to the other, and can only become receptive in a balanced way to the two aspects at the same time after long efforts of work on oneself.

From this point of view, the lower centers can be considered as divided into two parts, positive and negative; but this division looks somewhat different according to which of the centers is in question. At first sight, the distinction seems clear enough, and indeed it is for the moving center and the instinctive center; but it is much less clear for the emotional center and the intellectual center.

On the level of the intellectual center, which constates, analyzes, compares, associates and coordinates by means of the data recorded on the rolls, the activity of the mind results in an affirmative or negative judgment—yes or no. Usually one or the other predominates, and this judgment is the basis of our actions. We think we are choosing and deciding. Yet there is nothing there but a mechanical perception based on present or remembered external data. There is no free choice, no decision which really comes from us and is taken on behalf of a higher individual presence, that is, of an autonomous and permanent I with an understanding and aims of its own in life. At most there are little transitory aims belonging to the personage of the moment, conditioned by the mental associations available on the rolls. And when, in the working of the mental function, the positive and the negative balance precisely, we remain in a state of indecision.

But because in ordinary man there is nothing above the mental function that can take charge of his automatic judgments and put them to his own use, these constatations themselves are what pass for choice and decision. This is how the mind usurps a power to which it has no right, and which as matters stand can only be opposed by the contrary desires of the emotional center or the laziness of the moving center. What we commonly call a strong-willed man is a man whose strong, active, clearly-structured mind has learned to enlist the support of his desires and to bring the moving center into its service. But there is no will of his own, none of the free choice of a real individuality endowed with knowledge and pursuing through life aims which are objectively his own. There is nothing but the effect of circumstances on the automatic functioning of the mentality and a well-structured human machine. Such a man, contrary to what he generally thinks, is merely the result and plaything of influences independent of himself.

On the level of the instinctive center, the division between positive and negative is very clear; at least it would be if we were more attentive to the inner life of our organism. The perceptions of this center, positive or negative, pleasant or unpleasant, are all necessary for maintaining, guiding and directing our life.

When they have not been interfered with, the positive, pleasant, agreeable perceptions (sense perceptions and bodily perceptions of taste, smell, touch, or pure air, of the quality of food and of temperature) all point to salutary conditions of existence. The opposite, negative perceptions all signal harmful conditions.

In addition, there are instinctive perceptions connected with other parts of the machine, most often emotional and sometimes intellectual. These may either belong to the higher parts of our instinctive center, where we suspect their existence without knowing them too well, or they may come from the instinctive part of the emotional or the intellectual center. (We shall say more about them later.)

But the abnormal conditions of life and the education of man today insure that these perceptions are always more or less seriously muddled up. In any case, man today is no longer able to account rightly for these various perceptions. Fortunately, the instinctive center, which works at the level of the lower story in the shadowy depths of the machine, has retained a close relationship with the elemental forces of life which animate it. If the disturbances from outside become too threatening, the instinctive function by itself restores the balance—the man falls ill or his activity is stopped. But if the imbalance goes too far, it may lead to death.

At the level of the moving center, the division into two parts, positive and negative, is very simple. This center can be active or inactive—there can be movement or relaxation. It can also be neutral, at rest.

The moving center is a center with a tendency to be passive—it seldom acts on its own and is willing to obey whatever is asked of it, no matter what the source of the demand. On account of this naturally passive disposition, this center, even more than the others, is inclined to be lazy; a man often has to "force himself" to act. In an ordinary man, whose centers and personages function disconnectedly, these demands on the moving center may come from various sources, sometimes in agreement with each other, sometimes contradictory; its action then becomes chaotic, or else, if there is too much disorder, the moving center takes refuge in its natural laziness.

A very good example with which we can measure this disorder of the moving activity is provided by spoken language, which belongs to the moving center and is put by it at the disposal of the other centers—above all of the intellectual center, in association with which it has progressively been developed.

Left in peace, the moving center would in fact be available—that is, not merely inactive, but in a state of availability where the higher part of the center, which is eager to serve, would remain highly receptive and ready to respond.

But in his ordinary state a man does not have such a degree of availability. Even apart from any actual activity, his moving center is constantly appealed to by the personage of the moment, and takes an attitude corresponding to it. Thus each of us has a whole repertory of attitudes, always the same ones, indicative of the personage who is present, and observation of which, if there is a need for it, can bring the personage to light. And due to the existence of reciprocal and automatic associations, the artificial reproduction of any given attitude tends to bring the corresponding personage to the surface. This automatic "signaling" in two directions between inner states and outer attitudes occurs incessantly in social behavior without our being aware of it: it is part of the human machine and its conditioning.

The negative side of the moving center, its genuine inactivity, is letting go or relaxation. This does not come about by itself, but requires an active and voluntary giving up of any demand upon the moving center by the other centers. There are various degrees of relaxation according to whether there is a greater or lesser degree of disconnection, and three principal aspects of it stand out which have an immediately practical use, although in fact there may be many others. These are the basic "attitudes" on which can be established the physical tranquility needed for the inner searching for a relation to the higher parts in oneself. As such, they are the preliminary stage of exercises in contemplation and meditation. The first of these aspects is simply the complete tranquilization of the body in a natural and stable posture without the slightest strain.

It is by sensation that we are informed about all these states of our moving center. Of all the impressions we have of our inner life, physical sensation is undoubtedly what is most immediately accessible to us, the most "concrete," and the least given to fallacious imagination. To recognize it is easy: the sensation of ourselves is there or not there depending on whether we are turned toward ourselves or attracted outside, and this is why it can be considered one of the best tests for verifying the reality of efforts toward self-awareness.

Without knowing it, we lead our ordinary life with a constant sensing which informs us all the time about our postures, gestures and movements, but only rises to the conscious level when something unexpected and disturbing happens. Constantly forgetting ourselves, we also lose at the same time the sensation of ourselves. Reconstituting this sensing has to be part of any endeavor to awake to oneself.

At the level of the emotional center, the division into two parts, positive or negative, may appear simple at first, but in fact it is much more complex. It might seem at first sight that we have a whole array of "positive feelings"—joy, sympathy, affection—and "negative feelings"—fear, jealousy, boredom, irritation.

As a matter of fact, as we have seen, ordinary man, in spite of what he believes, has nothing which could be called feeling and as such calls him to an unchanging quality in his individual life. He only has emotions tied to the expression and preservation of each of his ever-changing personages, which are unrelated to his true individuality. In his ordinary waking state every real feeling is disconnected from the flow of life and, just like the higher I, remains in a state of sleep.

According to whether the impression of inner or outer events is taken as favorable or unfavorable, desirable or undesirable relative to the personage present, a pleasant or unpleasant emotion arises. But if, a moment later, there is a change of personage, the same impression has every chance of being taken differently. Thus in ordinary man, his "mood" is constantly changing, and according to the personage of the moment the same emotional impulses change from positive to negative or vice versa. All our pleasant emotions such as joy, sympathy and confidence, may degenerate at any moment into sadness, aversion, jealousy, doubt, and so on. The expression of these disagreeable emotions, which man cannot usually keep to himself, only serves to reinforce them needlessly and to spread their negativity around him. That is one of the reasons why the struggle against the outer expression of these negative emotions is one of the first points from which work on oneself can usefully begin.

From the moment it has become possible to begin such work, the situation itself begins to change. The man who has undertaken real work on himself begins in his moments of presence to measure himself "objectively" and to evaluate events in relation to his real self and no longer in relation to the use which his personages make of them. On the one hand, the illusory nature of his ordinary emotions, whether positive or negative, is gradually revealed to him, while at the same time he sees the conditional quality of his personages. On the other hand, a different evaluation of his impressions becomes possible for him through a relationship to the I that is awakening. Alongside his emotions, he can then distinguish real moral sufferings, belonging to the emotional center, and as much a part of his life as physical suffering, such as sickness, pain and death. He has numerous sorrows, fears, and anxieties which cannot be avoided. And above all, as he becomes more able to see himself, the inadequacies and failures which he records no longer arouse regrets and resolutions or impulses "to correct himself" but the true "subjective" feeling of remorse of conscience. For all these reasons, the awakening and evolution of man, if they bring—thanks to the awakening of a true feeling of self and of inner conscience—real impressions of joy and satisfaction, are equally and constantly associated with real impressions of sorrow and remorse insofar as his evolution is not complete.

Hope for a genuine change can come only with the realization of a true I, of a stable unified Presence, in which the center of gravity of one's life has been permanently established. The shocks and the real positive or negative feelings of ordinary life are not suppressed as such, but, for a man who has realized this permanence, they no longer affect his presence at the same level. Actually, this change takes place in the region of the higher emotional center, and is accompanied by the true feelings, which have no negativity, in this center. The feelings constantly induced by life, which would otherwise become subjective emotions, are correctly placed within an objective framework. There is no negative feeling at the level of the higher emotional center, nor, as we have seen, any negativity within this center, any more than there is in the higher intellectual center.

Neither is there normally any negativity in the sex center. In this respect it is analogous to the two higher centers with which its higher parts work. Sexual impressions, in the proper sense of the term, just like true feelings, are positive to a greater or lesser degree or are indifferent. This is true in the case of a man who has developed his higher levels and possesses a true I. In the sex center, either there is attraction accompanied by a pleasant impression or else there is nothing, indifference. On the ordinary level, it may appear to be otherwise; but observation shows that this is due to interferences of the other centers which are constantly taking place at the lower level of the sex center—nowhere is the bad work of centers as habitual as in the sex center. The negativity attributed to sex impressions derives entirely, in fact, from the negative impressions belonging to the other centers, but transferred to the sex center. These interferences are produced especially by the negative parts of the emotional center and the instinctive center: certain sexual stimuli (ideas, recollections, actions) can thus provoke unpleasant emotions or sensations. Moreover the ensuing repressions and refusals are often considered (and a "good" upbringing contributes to this) to be proofs of "courage" or "virtue," whereas they are merely aberrations.

The structure of the ordinary centers has still another characteristic feature. This is that the centers are composed of three parts or aspects, both on their positive as well as their negative side. These three parts are the reflection, on the level of the centers, of the fundamental threefold structure of every living entity, which is again a distant reflection of the three primary forces. Thus each center is made up of a selective (or intelligent) aspect, an affective (or motivating) aspect and a mechanical (or executive) aspect. We generally know only one of the aspects of each center, and then very unequally according to which centers we are or are not used to living in by preference. The other aspects are more or less inert, asleep, or hidden in darkness. But self-observation enables us little by little to see what was in the dark and soon to discover unexpected possibilities. Further, there are still more complications in that each of these parts of the centers is, in turn, subdivided into three aspects, and so on: but this sort of analysis is of no more help for the task we have undertaken.

Each of these parts or aspects of centers has its own characteristics, its own role, and functions with its own particular kind of attention. The mechanical aspect of each of the centers is automatic and involuntary: it reacts by opposition or acceptance with a reactive, automatized attention, changing the object of attention at each moment according to the circumstances. The motivational aspect of centers is personal and variable; it functions by attraction or repulsion, for or against the ongoing activity of the center (moving, feeling, thinking) with a captive—even blocked—attention which is self-perpetuating either on account of an identification, an interest, or a revulsion which seems at the time to be insuperable. The selective aspect of centers is "intelligence." It operates by comparison and choice, depending on a knowledge which endows it with a certain logical foresight; thus it eliminates, it coordinates, perhaps it even innovates; and this work requires an active attention which is not maintained without a certain effort.

All of this forms a complex whole of which some parts that seem alike are basically quite different, while different centers can give rise to exactly the same manifestations. Whoever tries to observe himself may find this disconcerting; how to differentiate, for example, between what arises from the emotional part of the intellectual center (such as the satisfaction of learning) and what comes from the intellectual part of the emotional center (such as the appreciation of knowledge)? For this a clear vision of oneself is necessary, and the first step toward that is to find in oneself what function is directing at that moment. I am in the act of . . . (learning or thinking, liking or appreciating, doing or acting): this shows which center I am in. Next, to try to see what characterizes this way of functioning—an intellectual, emotional or instinctive-moving mode. Here, among the various possible criteria, undoubtedly the most accessible is to take it from the point of view of attention. Without attention, or with a dispersed, wandering attention, we are in the mechanical part of the center; with a captive attention, held by what we are doing (the action, the emotion or the reflection), we are in the emotional part; with an attention controlled and maintained by persistent choice, we are in the intellectual part. At the beginning only the most typical situations, those which leave no room for doubt, should be considered. All situations which admit doubt must at first be put aside. Then very soon, with experience, it will become possible to see oneself more clearly and to be less misled about what is going on within oneself.

Another fundamental difference between the centers is the great disparity which exists between their speeds, that is, the respective speeds of their functions. We are so used to this phenomenon that we do not notice it unless our attention is drawn to it. But as soon as we are told about it, and begin to observe ourselves, this fact becomes obvious. The easiest observation is that which tries to compare the speed of the moving and intellectual functions. Our moving center must be informed by the intellectual center: but when it has learned what to do, and how to do it, the intelligence and speed of its work go beyond any intellectual control. In cases where the work is a bit complicated, such as driving a car, using machine tools, or running along a winding path, continuous observation by the intellect is clearly impossible—the intellect cannot keep up with such a tempo. For observation to become possible, either we must accept that a great deal escapes us (otherwise there is a risk of an accident) or we must slow down enormously the work of the moving center, or even stop it. Similar comparative observations may be made in regard to the other functions. In particular, it is well known that the instinctive center works at a prodigious speed, and that the rapidity of the impressions it brings us or of the work which it accomplishes (in connection with hunger, thirst, or digestion, for example) is almost miraculous for anyone who tries to analyze it.

The slowest center is in fact the intellectual center. Next, and much faster, comes the moving center. The instinctive center, although it works in close relation with the moving center, is still faster. The fastest of all is the emotional center, whose impressions, when it works normally, appear to us to be instantaneous; but in our ordinary state, it most often works at lower speeds—the speeds of the instinctive and moving centers.

Calculations based on the respective times taken up by analogous periods (such as the cycle of breathing, or the cycle of day and night) on the different levels of life show that the apparent relationship of time on two adjacent levels is of the order of 1 to 30,000.* Applied to the speeds of functioning of the centers, this relationship would show that the moving center, for example, functions 30,000 times faster than the intellectual center.

We have the habit of taking intellectual time as absolute time, although it is the slowest, and of referring everything to this standard. This, by the way, is rather significant, for the perception of times is an "ideally subjective" phenomenon, which is peculiar to each particular form of life. If it is said that the time of the moving center is 30,000 times quicker than that of the intellectual center, it can equally well be said that in the same lapse of intellectual time, the moving center can perform 30,000 times more operations, or again it can be said that the time of the moving center is 30,000 times longer than that of the intellectual center. The time of the instinctive center will be $30{,}000^2$ times faster and that of the emotional center (at least in its normal functioning) will be $30{,}000^3$ times faster.

It is hard to believe that there are such differences in speed between the various functions within one and the same organism, yet this explains a number of phenomena. Thus the sum total of information, transformations and reactions that the instinctive center contributes in one second becomes comprehensible if, knowing that it functions $30{,}000^2$ times faster, we calculate that this one second represents more than twenty years of intellectual time. It appears even that these faster centers, far from being fully employed, are resting (or sleeping) most of the time, so that, from this angle too, man has many more resources than he generally believes.

Last but not least, we come to the important point which self-observation can enable us to discover, namely, the large

* Cf. Ouspensky, *In Search of the Miraculous*, p. 332.

part played by the wrong work of centers and the obstacle this raises for our evolution.

This wrong work has three aspects which, moreover, interfere with and have repercussions on each other.

On the one hand, in ordinary man there is a slowing down of the lower centers, especially the emotional center, which work far below their normal speed.

On the other hand, the functions are constantly putting out an excessive expenditure for whatever work they have to do, and this results in a considerable waste of energy.

Finally (but this is more difficult to catch in ourselves), substitutions are continually taking place. The centers substitute for each other, with the result that some do not do the work they should do, and it is carried out by the others. There are also substitutions of one level of functioning for another; certain centers (particularly on account of slowing down) begin to use the energy of other centers, an energy which is not suitable for them, and with which their proper function is done badly, or with which they begin to do useless, even harmful, work.

In observing our functions in ourselves, and consequently the work of centers, we can come to know little by little their correct work and their incorrect work.

In a normal man, normally developed and in good health, each center does its own work—the work which it is destined to do and for which it is best qualified. Any intrusion of another center in this work and every use of another function is less effective or leads to a loss of quality. There are even some situations in life from which a man can extricate himself only with the help of the appropriate center; if, at such times, another center takes its place, this leads to interference, maladjustment and often the most embarrassing consequences such as entanglements, error, confusion, abortive effort, accident, destruction—the outcome is unpredictable. These substitutions take place, however, in nearly all men, because man's development is almost always unbalanced. Sometimes the substitutions are even necessary to fill lapses of functioning, to cope with certain situations and to preserve the continuity of life. But if they become habitual—and too often this is the case—they become harmful. By interfering with correct working they not only disguise what is lacking (thus preventing us from seeing it and taking steps to correct it) but they also make it possible for each center to avoid its own immediate tasks and do, not what it has to do, but what it finds more pleasant at the moment. Indeed, all the centers are more or less lazy, dreamy and subject to opportunist or vagabond tendencies that remove their willingness to accept voluntarily the tasks required of them.

Thus any man considered normal can already observe in himself the attempts (or, more exactly, the pretensions) of the intellectual center to feel, the attempts of the emotional center to think, the attempts of the moving center to think and to feel. In the case of an unbalanced man, the substitution of one or several centers for each other is more or less continuous and leads precisely to what is called "an unbalanced state of mind" or "neurosis." Each center tries in some way to pass its work on to another center, and at the same time tries to do the work of a center for which it is not fitted.

It is important to learn to recognize in oneself the characteristic signs of these substitutions of centers for each other. It is difficult and takes a long time to observe, for nothing in us is better disguised. Each of the centers, when it takes the place of another in this way, nevertheless brings with it into a realm not normally its own the functional characteristics which belong to it and by which it is recognizable.

When the emotional center works for another center, it brings with it its sensitivity, its speed, its intensity and above all an egocentric quality that gives it away more than any other sign does. When it works instead of the intellectual center, it produces nervousness, feverish and unneccessary haste, exactly where, on the contrary, calm judgment and deliberation are called for. When it works instead of the moving center, it produces impulsiveness and a tendency to be carried away rather than making the right movement. In the place of the instinctive center, it produces exaggerated effects and too much or too little activity.

When the intellectual center works for another center, it produces discussion, equivocation, and slowing down. It also brings with it its taste for dreaming and imagination. Finally, it produces a certain inflexibility, for, on the one hand, it is the slowest of all the centers and, on the other, it is not subtle enough to perceive the particularities and more delicate aspects of a situation, still less to see how the situation progressively changes. Thus its interference ends up by producing inappropriate or faulty reactions, attitudes which are rigid, too generalized and often completely fixed. It is in fact incapable of understanding the nuances and subtleties of most events. Situations that appear completely different to the moving or emotional center seem identical to the intellectual center, and its decisions are not the same as the other centers would have taken.

Thought is unable to understand shades of feeling, and with it cold calculation takes the place of living emotion. Thus, when a man merely reasons about another person's feelings, even if he tries to imagine what they are, he experiences nothing himself and what the other is experiencing is for him non-existent. The same is true in the instinctive realm—the man who has eaten his fill does not understand the man who is hungry; but for the latter there is no doubt about the reality of his hunger and the other man's arguments or decisions—that is to say, his thought—generally seem incomprehensible.

The intellectual center is neither capable of substituting for the moving center nor of controlling movements—sensation does not exist for it, sensation is a dead thing for which it substitutes visualization. It is easy to find examples: if a man tries to make his gestures intentionally, by thinking about them, directing each movement with his thought, he will see at once that the tempo and quality of his work changes. Whether using a typewriter or driving his car, he begins (as when he was learning) to move slowly and make one mistake after another—thought cannot keep up with the normal pace of the moving center. In another field, spectator sports, as opposed to the practice of sports, is also an example of the substitution of the intellectual function (and also of its tendency to dream) for the activity of the instinctive and motor centers.

The moving center, when it tries to take over the work of another center, produces its regularity, its power, its submissiveness, its talent for imitation, but it also brings with it its laziness, its inertia, and its inclination for what is habitual and automatic. Often it does the work of the intellectual center, or, still more often, continues (by inertia) work that the intellectual center had begun; in fact, the intellectual center, while carrying out some work which it has undertaken, often allows itself to be distracted by something that captures its attention—sometimes by some other useful work, more often by dreams or imagination; then the moving center takes on the work instead, or continues alone with the work that the two centers had started together. This results, for example, in mechanical reading or mechanical listening where we read words (sometimes aloud) or hear phrases without understanding their meaning: we remain unconscious of them and do not even remember them. The attempts of the moving center to feel are perhaps less obvious, yet they also play a very important role; for example, they introduce mechanicalness and habits into human relationships, with all that this entails.

But nowhere is the wrong work of centers so habitual and such a serious obstacle as at the level of the sex center. The sex center functions with the finest energy produced by the human organism; it is the most highly refined and has the greatest intensity and speed. In normal conditions, it establishes a harmonious relationship with all the other centers and makes them participate in its creative activity, the highest activity which is normally the lot of every created individuality at whatever level or levels it lives. Consequently, the sex center reflects all their qualities and all their deficiencies. But in the usual conditions of man's life, it is quite otherwise: the relation of the sex center to the others is established badly or not at all. This is due to the wrong work of centers, since in most of them—and especially the emotional center—only the mechanical part functions and at a speed and with a quality quite inferior to their normal working. Only in exceptional moments, when it sometimes succeeds in re-establishing temporarily an almost normal rhythm and relationship, does the sex center function in a self-directed way. At best it succeeds in establishing a link with one or another of the centers, and then it expresses itself through its function. Most often it remains completely passive, and the other centers make use of its energy for their benefit. This then gives their functioning a quite unaccustomed intensity and exaggeration colored by the polarity proper to the individual, and the resulting impression of intense life is often pursued in the form of "sexual deviations" such as eroticism, romanticism, sado-masochism and all their minor derivatives. As a general rule, the sex center functions only at its lower mechanical level, closely connected to the three levels of the instinctive and moving centers, and together they form a whole (where the sex center is the neutralizing element) which is sufficiently balanced for the purposes of everyday life. Sometimes also the sex center joins up with the lower emotional level of the feeling center. But it is altogether impossible that such a combination—except on the organic level—would allow full play to the creative functions allotted to this center at the various levels of life possible to man. When a man commits himself to work on himself with the aim of developing his higher parts, it is almost always necessary to put the sex function back in its proper place. Its energy—which is the finest—and a proper functioning of the center are indispensable to this work: and if it proves to be impossible to put the function back in its right place, there is then an insurmountable obstacle to all progress.

To sum up, the wrong functioning and interferences of the centers, which are habitual, represent such a waste of energy and loss of quality that for most people a whole preliminary work of putting in order is generally necessary before real work on oneself can begin. To economize the energy of our organism and to balance and regulate the work of the centers whose functions constitute our life is the first stage in re-establishment of a rhythm of right work and of contact with the higher centers which is the basis for all evolution of man.

Underlying the wrong functioning of the human machine and the rupture between the centers used for ordinary life and the two higher centers is the insufficient development of the lower centers. It is precisely this lack of development of the lower centers, or their faulty functioning, which prevents man from making use of his higher centers by hindering the establishment of connections with them.

But if by his personal work and the appropriate efforts (which are only possible in a school) a man begins to develop his lower centers and to balance them, the emotional center may find its normal level of functioning again; and, as it becomes purified and more developed, contact is established with the higher emotional center. Later, through this, a new contact may come to be established with the higher intellectual center. Contrary to what some modern disciplines are attempting, no direct contact is possible between the lower intellectual center and the higher intellectual center. The axis of development of the human being is founded in an emotional development, an evolution of the feeling of self—its awakening, its development, and transcendence.

Essence and personality

ONE of the most important points in self-study is the distinction, in our motivations and functionings, between what belongs to us, comes from ourselves, is a part of our own nature, and what is foreign to us, comes from the environment and represents only a loan.

From this point of view, we are divided into two parts. One part is what we are born with; it contains the seed of the qualities rightfully belonging to us—our capacities, our incapacities and more generally everything that has been given to us as our own. We shall call it our "essence"—a term which cannot fail to arouse discussion in present circumstances but which is here restored to its original meaning, the one which is used by Gurdjieff. Essence, almost entirely potential at birth, develops to a certain degree afterward and becomes what we shall also call man's "being"—his inner being, the core of his "individuality." This development, to the extent it takes place, is the development of our real being; it corresponds in degree to our experience of reality in the world, and by this fact it is almost entirely real (keeping in mind among other things that it still contains an unrealized potential).

The other part is what we have acquired—all our knowledge and most of what attracts us, most of our behavior. This is non-existent at birth and is formed in us gradually due to all that the surrounding conditions superimpose on us. For this reason, Gurdjieff uses the term "personality" (from Latin *persona*, a mask) for this part of us. Its development is as a rule only remotely connected (according to what we have taken in) with the reality of the surrounding world and in certain cases may even be made up almost entirely of imaginary notions.

In an ordinary man, these two parts are almost always so inextricably mixed as to be indistinguishable. However, both of them are there, each with its own life and "significance." Both are necessary for life; and if a man wants to know himself, to know "his life," he must first become able to differentiate between them in himself.

A man's personality is "what does not belong to him"; that is, he mirrors the movements, words, and the language which have been taught him, all the traces of external impressions recorded in the memory of his different centers, sensations, the feelings he has learned, the ideas he has acquired by imitation or by suggestion—all this is personality.

It can also be said that personality is formed out of the contents of the centers, that is, by what is inscribed on the recording apparatus connected to each center, as well as by the mechanisms that link the centers together. There are mechanisms which make associations between different records on the same roll or between records on different rolls, and there are buffering mechanisms which have the effect of preventing contradictory records from being made or from being recalled at the same time.

Personality develops as a result of external circumstances (place, time and environment) and it depends almost entirely on them. Even though the conditionings which it is made up of may be very strong, it can be altered more or less deeply by a change in these conditions, and such changes may be almost complete and sometimes very quick. It can be lost, can deteriorate, be corrected or strengthened.

Essence, on the contrary, is what is innate. In other words, it is the particular gifts and traits peculiar to each man, his patrimony, put into his charge to make it "grow" in life. One man has a gift for music, another has none; one has the gift of languages, another has not; one has a taste for travel and escape, another likes to sit at home or is a recluse; one is straightforward and sincere, another is devious and suspicious; one oversimplifies everything, the other makes everything too complicated. The totality of these particular traits is essence. Their development in the course of life may take place or may not take place. They may be accentuated or modified. This development of essence, its growth, represents the "being" of man. Essence and being in man are "what are really his," what really belong to him and go with him everywhere. As opposed to personality, essence cannot be lost and cannot be modified without, at least, the tacit consent of the man in question. In a weak being "who lets himself be carried away" by the surroundings he is in, essence may be smothered or even altogether crushed almost without his realizing it; or, on the contrary, it may be liberated and rebalanced. But in any case it cannot be developed and changed without a man's conscious and persevering participation. Changes in essence are slow and call for much more work, more time and more depth than changes in personality.

Essence and personality have as their support a third constituent of man: his organic body. This is the instrument through which all the exchanges which make life possible take place. These are the three basic elements given to man. Each of them has its center of gravity in one of the principal centers of man. The center of gravity of the body is the moving center; the center of gravity of essence is the emotional center; and the center of gravity of the personality is the intellectual center.

In the natural order of man's life, these three parts develop independently; they only come into conflict accidentally and are only occasionally connected together; no real connections are established between them. The establishment of real connections can only come as the result of a specially directed work of man on himself, and carrying out such work is the first step toward achieving unity and individuality.

His threefold constitution makes this individuality possible for man, with the quality of presence that goes with it, because it allows him to participate fully on his level in the fundamental interactions of life's creative forces; but since his three parts are independent of each other by nature, individuality is not given to man at birth. It can only be attained as a result of a long work on himself. Knowledge of the body, essence and personality is needed to accomplish this work.

At the beginning of life, a human being is body and essence; personality is still potential and without form—a child behaves as he really is; his desires, his tastes, what he likes and what he doesn't like express his being such as it is.

But as soon as the necessity to face life arises, personality begins to grow. It is formed in part by intentional external influences (what we call education), in part by involuntary imitation of adults by the child himself, and partly also by the child's "resistance" to what is around him and by efforts to protect (and to disguise if necessary) what he feels to be himself and to be his own—that which is "real" in him, his essence.

In one way or another, "consciously" or "unconsciously," whether wished for or not, the human being acquires, little by little, many tastes, feelings, ideas and judgments which are artificial, that is, which are not related to those that would be natural to him and would express his own essence. All these traits acquired by education, by imitation, by opposition and by imagination come to take up more and more room; and to the degree that this artificial personality increases, essence manifests more and more seldom, more and more indirectly and feebly.

In childhood, essence still holds a major place. What comes

from outside interacts directly with essence, is combined with it or opposes it, so to speak, "in equal parts" and is accepted or refused. And finally essence confronts the outside impressions without really blending with them, creating a complex still permeated with the essential nature. This is how traits acquired in very early childhood leave an indelible mark on the child (and the man) and form what one may call, in effect, his second nature. For this very reason, it is valuable for a man who wishes to know himself to go back as far as possible in his childhood memories and rediscover tastes and feelings there, if he can, through which the characteristics of his essence may come to light more easily.

Later on, the characteristics which come into existence draw less and less upon essence; they are made up of acquired traits in whose formation essence has played a smaller and smaller part, and soon essence, for most people, only gives a broad coloration (a life style or general tendency) which tints the entire personality with that particular shade and permeates the way of living—unless, in the adult man, even this coloration has disappeared, in which case nothing is left of his essence, and such a man is no more than a personality of facades and lies. For, in relation to himself, essence is the truth in man and personality is the lie.

A grown man does not naturally have more consciousness of his being and his essence—self-consciousness—than a child does. But a very young child who has not yet learned other ways of feeling and of expressing himself or herself responds to life in conformity with his or her own nature, that is, with his or her essence. A child is still simple. An adult, on the contrary, has acquired an entire structure, a surface personality which covers all the parts of his own being and is only remotely connected with himself—he has become dual. And he habitually answers to life according to this surface personality without his essence being brought into these responses. Even if he wishes his essence to come in, it can no longer do so without his making a special effort which has to be renewed each time. Personality has taken up all the room in him, and, in ordinary life, it answers by itself to every call: it has finally substituted itself for essence. And this substitution is the principal cause of man's mechanical state and the reason why he cannot free himself from it; it is also the natural consequence of the law of least effort, the law which governs all that lives in the involutionary current.

This substitution comes about unconsciously as a man grows up, due to his natural inertia, and because of a lack of sincerity with himself—a complacency constantly reinforced by the usual education. Our functions are ceaselessly answering to life, but it is easier for us to reply as the outer world requires than to experience our actual situation and reply "out of one's soul and conscience." Eventually, it becomes easier to go back to answering in the way that was already learned than to question everything each time and adapt the response according to what one feels inwardly to be right, as if for the first time on each occasion. The formation of habits leads to this taking the easy way out. Thus "by force of circumstances" various personages are built up in us who get into the habit of dealing with each of the usual situations in which we find ourselves. Because it is easier to imagine than to act and easier to believe than to look and see, these personages gradually get saturated with illusions which make contact with reality more and more remote. And because these personages have such contradictory relationships, both with each other and with reality, that there is a danger of generating destructive shocks, this entire structure is protected by a system of "buffers." The structure bears our name: "Mr. So-and-so," Peter, Paul, John or Jack, the name we give out and by which others know us, without suspecting it does not correspond to what we really are. It is the form in which we appear to others and are of use to them—they do not generally expect anything more.

Moreover, this formation, our personality, is jealously guarded by a "feeling" which is supported by them as much as by ourselves, namely, a hypersensitive self-love, which insures that the formation and its functionings manifest through each of our personages according to rigidly fixed ideas and images.

Thus, in the great majority of cases, nothing that we see in a man is really his own. Without his knowing it he is a living lie. His personality claims to know all about himself, about life, God, the universe, everything; but in himself, in his essence, in his being, he knows nothing about any of it and has not verified anything. It is not true that he really possesses any of this knowledge which he attributes to himself; he has only picked it up from his surroundings. Nor does he possess a single one of the qualities that he believes himself to have; he has only imagined them without taking the trouble to test them by experience.

The result of this development of personality and its progressive substitution for essence is that essence receives less and less of the elements necessary for its growth and it generally stops developing at a very early age. The being of an adult, even one who is intellectual and very cultured, is often arrested between the ages of six and twelve. Such a man may write books, become wealthy or govern a nation, but he is little more than personality; his essence no longer manifests except in his instinctive life and sometimes in his simplest emotions. It is possible to make an experimental confirmation of this relationship between personality and essence. One of the two can be put to sleep or separated from the other for a certain time by means of hypnosis or by certain drugs. Such means cause one (generally essence) to remain while the other is put to sleep, or they cause two beings to appear and coexist, whose interests, tastes and aims are quite different and whose development is not the same. These techniques were employed in certain Eastern schools, and similar effects are possible through modern neurochemistry.

It is exceptional for being and personality to develop harmoniously. In practice, they almost always develop unequally. With cultured people, it is personality which is developed; the whole of civilization, science, art, philosophy, politics, is nothing but a manifestation of personality. Among such people the being remains infantile, or stupid. Among people living in contact with nature, and in difficult conditions, being has more opportunity to grow, but personality generally is too little developed; they have no formal education, instruction, culture or knowledge.

In fact, for work on oneself, for right development of a true individuality, of a permanent I, and later, for going beyond this I, a harmonious development of essence and personality is indispensable; the development of personality to a certain degree is as necessary as a certain growth of essence. Without a sufficient stock of data and knowledge that are acquired and "not his own" a man cannot undertake real work on himself on the way of Understanding. Other ways are open to him, such as the way of the "fakir," or the way of the monk, which do not require any intellectual development. At the same time, without a sufficient development of essence, real work on oneself is not possible. If essence is too little developed, a relatively long preliminary work is indispensable to bring it to the desired level, and this work will be fruitless if essence is rotten inside or if it has contracted some irremediable defect. Such cases are very common; an abnormal development of personality often stops the development of essence at such a low level that it becomes a small, deformed thing from which nothing can be expected. It even happens frequently that a man's essence dies, while his body and personality are still alive. Indeed, almost all the people one sees in the streets of any large city are practically empty inside and are actually already dead. It is fortunate for us that we cannot see this and know nothing about it; for such a sight, with its consequences, would be unbearable for us. People who become able to see it have first as a rule gained sufficient preparation to bear this vision.

Thus the common tragedy of man in our civilization is that his personality has taken the place of being. It forms a shell that isolates the essence and prevents anything from reaching it any more. It is personality which receives all the demands, impressions and shocks of life; it responds in its way, and directs everything according to its own rules and for its own benefit. It responds, in conformity with its structure, in a way that is reflexive, superficial and immediate; personality reacts. It lives on and feeds off these reactions, every one of which reinforces its structure and strengthens its conditioning, which is maintained as a whole by a highly sensitive emotional apparatus, namely, its self-love.

Essence is not able to react. When an impression reaches it, essence confronts it immediately with lived experience, "understands it" and, according to this understanding, responds.

Essence lives and feeds on this process of understanding and response by which it assimilates the content of new experience; it is thus that essence grows. But its way of responding is much slower than the reacting of personality. In man's usual state, personality seizes on an impression as soon as it is received; it reacts immediately. Nothing has time to reach essence, which in a certain sense is robbed, "short-circuited." Each time, by however little, personality grows and essence declines. Finally, personality forms a matrix that takes up all the space, while essence sleeps and atrophies inside.

Deep down in a man, as long as it is not yet too late, a feeling may appear now and then and warn him of the situation he is in—if he turns himself toward himself, he may feel that his inner responses, those of his essence, are truly his own and are sincere, whereas his habitual reactions, coming from his personality, seem to belong to an alien world outside himself and to obey rules or laws of this outer world which are not his own. These reactions have no connection with what he feels to be himself, and can just as easily be found to be acceptable as to be a betrayal. They are what they are, but in any case they have no sincerity whatever in relationship to himself. To make room for his inner conscience, to have this need of sincerity toward himself, is the first quality necessary for anyone who wishes to undertake work for self-knowledge. This is what education should teach a child first of all; and for a man who wishes to know himself, this is the best guide at the beginning—at least, if he is still capable of listening to it and inclining toward himself with real love, a love for his essence—if he is capable of love of self. Love of self, the "good" egoism for essence and being, is analogous to self-love for personality.

Usually, man is completely unaware of this situation and, if his life goes by without too serious difficulties, he may never become aware of it. In order that something may change, his life must have disappointed him deeply enough to put into question his personality and the whole structure which it represents. To tell the truth, it would be enough for him to see himself as he is, inescapably to see himself reacting as he does to different circumstances with his contradictory personages, each of which lives for itself, egotistically, according to what pleases it with no regard for the rest, and even less for reality. To observe himself like that would make him see that something is false in his way of life and that his values are upside down. But a whole system of dampening devices—

excuses and buffers—well-established in his person prevent him from seeing this. The excuses are different from buffers in the sense that they are an artificial development, always changing, always different and depending on what is expedient at the moment. They may serve to express buffers, but they have no deep roots themselves other than the urgent need of each personage, when faced with his inadequacies and his contradictions, nevertheless always to be right; at the same time a certain intelligence is called for in order to always find "good" excuses. Buffers, on the contrary, are deeply imbedded inner devices, conditionings that are securely set in the structure of the personality and have grown along with it in order to damp down or camouflage or avoid the contradictions that make up the usual life of man—not only the contradictions between his different personages, but above all the contradictions between them and essence, arising from the abnormal predominance they have assumed. Buffers are permanent automatic mechanisms within the structure of personality, with whose development they have been built up. They have made its development possible and thus it is they who maintain its predominance.

This mechanism, however, is accidentally sometimes held in check by life—at times of violent shock (such as an accident or the death of a loved one) or at a moment of great disillusionment or of a new and unforeseen situation. If he is still able to have a certain sincerity, a man is then led to put in question again his usual way of living, and for a moment he feels a need to "understand." A special interest awakes in him to understand the causes of his situation, and for an instant he finds again in himself the wish to understand his being and to understand his life.

As a matter of fact, there is, in every man, a more or less buried side of him, asleep to a greater or lesser degree, that takes an interest in understanding himself and his life and, broadly speaking, life in general. Because of this special orientation toward a pole of fundamental interest, namely, the understanding of life, it may be called "magnetic center." It is not a "center" in the strict sense of the word, but only a center of interest, and, with the "magnetic apparatus" which corresponds to it, it belongs to personality, not to being. It is an interest for oneself, turned toward the understanding of oneself, whereas ordinarily all the interests of man are turned toward the externals. It is personality's interest in this latent demand for being that gets covered over—an interest turned toward himself, but nevertheless an interest like others; and a man generally has many interests of this sort in his personality. Such an interest for self, belonging to the person, is entirely different from self-consciousness, which develops in an awakened man and belongs to his being. However, interest in oneself, properly guided, may lead to self-consciousness.

This magnetic apparatus develops during upbringing so long as education is not too abnormal. It is formed out of the emotional or intellectual parts of personality which are sensitive to the need of essence, and sensitive also to certain outer influences that call to a man to "understand." Like everything else in personality, the apparatus is not active of itself, it only reacts to influences that reach it. But while the rest of personality reacts to influences of one kind created in life by life itself, the magnetic apparatus reacts to influences of another order, created outside of this life by conscious men for definite purposes. These influences come from the inner, esoteric circle of humanity, and are usually embodied in the form of doctrines, religious teachings, philosophical systems, works of art, and so on.

These influences are consciously let out into life with a definite aim, and they become mixed with influences of the first kind, coming from life. But they are conscious only in their origin. When they come into the great maelstrom of life, they fall under the law of accident and begin to act mechanically; in other words they are no longer adaptable—they may or may not act on a certain man, they may reach him or they may not—this depends only on him. In addition, as they undergo all sorts of changes and alterations in life in the process of transmission and interpretation, these influences of the second order are gradually reduced to influences of the first kind; that is, they are effectively merged.

Thus, in the case of a particular man, it all depends on the possibility of his receiving these two kinds of influences and differentiating between them. Their distribution at his level is not equal. In addition, everyone has a different sensitivity—one man is more attuned to influences from outside of life and he receives more of these, another receives less, while a third is hardly sensitive to them at all.

This is inevitable; it depends on the structure of essence and already belongs in the realm of fate. But if we consider the overall situation, the general rule, an average man living in average conditions, the conditions are nearly the same for everybody and one could say that the difficulty is more or less the same for all. It consists in separating the two kinds of influences. If a man upon receiving them does not separate them, does not see or feel their difference, their action on him will not be separated either; that is, they will act upon him in the same way, on the same level, will produce the same results and will not be able to lead him to any change. On the other hand, if a man at the moment of receiving these influences knows how to effect the necessary discrimination, and to put on one side the influences not created in life itself, it gradually becomes easier for him to separate them; after a certain time he cannot confuse them any more with ordinary influences and they begin to produce different results in him.

Therefore, among the very diverse forms that these influences can take, it is very important to know how to recognize what enables us to discriminate between the influences created within life itself and influences which come from a source outside of life. The special character of the second kind is that they call to us to turn to ourselves and to "understand." Thus, for each one of us, everything depends on our wish for understanding and on our capacity to recognize, among the different influences which reach us, those which can increase our understanding. This is the role which the magnetic center assumes in us. Many people, who may perhaps have suspected the importance of this distinction at the beginning of their life, are not even aware of the difference afterwards. But if a man is still able to be sufficiently sincere, or if an unexpected shock awakens this sincerity, influences of the second kind arouse a new interest in him when they touch him. They turn him for a moment toward essence, being, and all that concerns the understanding of what he is: his magnetic center begins to act in him for a moment.

The man who is sensitive to these influences accumulates the results that they induce in the various parts of his personality; he records them, associates them with each other, remembers them and after each new shock feels them all together. He himself is not able to grasp clearly what it is all about; he does not see the how or the why, and all his attempts to explain it to himself meet with failure. To start with, he calls this a "special interest," an "ideal" or "ideas" and so forth, but what is important is that this is in fact the first movement of a concern for the development of himself. The results of these influences which have begun to accumulate in him enlarge and progressively strengthen the magnetic center. At the same time it attracts all the related influences; and in this way it grows and little by little takes a separate place.

The magnetic center cannot take this place in man except

at the expense of other elements of his personality, because, being turned toward the inside while everything else is turned outward, it is not compatible with them; it is a question of one or the other. A struggle ensues between these two aspects of the person; this is always a difficult moment and the struggle can remain undecided forever. Nevertheless, if a man's magnetic center receives enough impressions, if the other sides of his personality, resulting from influences created in life, do not give too much resistance, and if the wish to be, rather than to make a good appearance, begins to awaken in him, the magnetic apparatus does start to have an influence on his orientation; it can become his principal interest and oblige the man to turn around and even bring him to set out toward the source of its influence. Essence and being enter into all this only to the degree that they are mixed with personality. Up to this point a man has no means of his own of distinguishing them and of working on them. But once his magnetic center has acquired enough force and is sufficiently developed, he begins to understand the idea of a way for development of his being, and to search for it.

This search for the way can take a very long time and can lead to nothing. It depends on the conditions, the circumstances, the strength of the magnetic center, and the strength and direction of other tendencies that are not interested in the search at all and can distract a man from his aim at the precise moment when the possibility of attaining it, that is, of finding the way, appears.

If the magnetic center works properly and if a man really searches, or even if, quite apart from an active search, he has the right kind of feeling, he may meet another man who knows the way and is connected, either directly or through intermediaries, with a center which is not subject to the law of accident, and from which the ideas come that have formed the magnetic center.

Here there are still many possibilities which leave the whole outcome in question. Nevertheless, at this point, the man has met—if the meeting is authentic—a third kind of influence which is direct, which is conscious, and which only acts from one man to another through lived experience and oral transmission. From this moment, what a man was searching for may begin to exist—a work adapted to self-development and the realization of his true being.

But, as its growth took place, the magnetic center may have been wrongly formed. It may include in itself contradictions and inner divisions. Influences coming from life may have entered it under the guise of influences coming from beyond life, or the higher influences may even have been perverted to the point of becoming the very opposite of what they were. A man whose magnetic center has been formed in this way may likewise be in search of a way of self-development. If he meets an authentic guide, a considerable preparatory work will be necessary before he is able to follow him, in order to neutralize the malformations of the magnetic center, and there is often a risk that such a man will not be able to accept this work. Moreover, such a man, more than others, is susceptible to setting out on paths and attaching himself to guides that, through error or imagination, will lead him in a totally different direction from the one he was seeking. Thus, without knowing it, he may be led very far from the real path, leading to diametrically opposite results to those he might otherwise have obtained. Fortunately, this rarely happens; for, although there are many false paths, in the great majority of cases they lead nowhere. A man simply beats about the bush on the same spot, thinking all the time he is getting somewhere.

To recognize whether a way is right or wrong is always very

difficult. Recognizing a wrong way is impossible except by knowing the right way. Those who are searching would like to be sure that the guide they have found is on the right way; however, no one can see above his own level and a student can never see the real level of his teacher. This is a law but most people do not know it; everyone wants to be taught by the highest master. At the beginning, the only hope of not being led in a wrong direction does not depend on appreciation (bound to be illusory) of the teacher, but upon recourse in oneself to a conscience which is still intact and to a sincere confrontation between it and what is indicated to one. If a man is not capable of such sincerity from the outset, there is every chance of his going astray, for the right way is rare and there are many wrong roads. Here, also, one must have gold to make gold.

At the same time that a right way aims at liberating a man from the prison of his personality, it also leads him to liberation from the laws which govern everyday life. Everything that belongs to personality is actually governed by the same laws as ordinary life—the laws of quantity, luck and accident. There is no true "destiny" in this field; there are only fortuitous circumstances and accidental meeting points. Even for man, the law of accident governs his everyday life and makes it to a very large extent unpredictable. The only hope for someone who wants to pursue an aim or follow a definite direction is to escape from this law, to become free of it. This assumes, first of all, that he has become aware of the law. It assumes further that he understands how to be free of it. Man is not only subject to individual accidents but also to collective accidents, governed by general laws. Not all the general laws are binding on a man; he can free himself from a great many of them, if he succeeds in freeing himself from imagination and buffers. And to accomplish all this the fundamental condition is that he free himself from personality.

The personality finds its sustenance in imagination and lying. When the lies in which man lives are fewer and the imagination has become weaker, personality itself will soon weaken and stop exercising control. Being is set free and a man can then come under the control either of his own "fate" or of a line of work directed by the will of another man. In this way, man can be brought to the point where will can be formed in him, a will capable of confronting both accident and, if necessary, "fate."

"Fate" is a word whose real meaning has been lost. In fact, fate is connected with essence and its development. The essence of each man has its own particular characteristics linked with the original influences (often held to be planetary or astral) which form his "type" and govern his principal tendencies. Different combinations of influences thus form the different essences. They also regulate sensitivity to the influences which are present in the environment; these latter change according to precise laws which may be experienced and known. The tendencies likewise change. Some develop of themselves, mechanically. Others, on the contrary, once they have appeared, weaken and atrophy unless they are given a stimulus regularly. For each man, the part related to his different possible tendencies, his particular sensitivity to each kind of influence, and the method of evolution corresponding to each tendency constitute his "destiny"—both his individual destiny and collective destiny, connected with the destiny of the whole to which he belongs. Man's "destiny" is usually not fulfilled because his being is not developed; personality has taken over its place and put man under the law of accident. Planetary influences are not able to reach essence until it frees itself from personality. This can happen mechanically; it is what occurs in communities, crowds and masses of people, when external influences, particularly planetary influences, are prevalent, and each individual has a natural tendency to lose all characteristics of his own. But for these influences to have a specific effect on a particular man, he has to have freed himself from the control of his personality, which is generally possible only through the work of a school.

Aside from his birth and often—though not always—his death, the part that the law of accident or the law of fate takes in a man's life really depends on the relationship between his personality and his essence. Those in whom personality is very strong are entirely, or almost entirely, under the law of accident; planetary influences only reach them at exceptional moments, or else indirectly, by reason of their being part of a crowd. But, simply because of their way of life (without the influence of a school being a factor), certain people live much more in their essence and only have a fragile personality. These people receive planetary influences much more directly and live much more under the law of their fate.

Whether it is better to live under the law of fate or under the law of accident is another question. This depends first of all on the point of view one takes in making such an evaluation. From the point of view of ordinary life fate may be better in certain cases and worse in others according to the useful qualities, respectively, of the essence which has been given and the personality which has been formed. Most often fate is better. From the point of view of being and the development of being the same alternatives exist but for entirely different reasons. To escape from the law of accident in order to return to the law of fate is obligatory for a man who is seeking self-realization. But there are some fates which it is better not to live through. As soon as the being becomes aware of this, an urgent sense of necessity appears at the same time to change his fate, to escape from it. While this is not impossible, it requires a very difficult, conscious work in conditions which are not always realized or are not realized for long enough to achieve the aim. In the case of such beings who finally experience failure and know it, it would have been better to remain under the law of accident. This is the real meaning of "hell." Fortunately, such situations are rare, because in the case of these people, the inner and outer obstacles are so strong that they are very seldom able to go far enough in real work on themselves.

The development of individuality and the appearance of a permanent "I," which is the first stage of the normal development of man, results in the growth of essence and the harmonious development of being and personality. This ought to be the aim of education—an education properly directed by teachers aware of the role they are responsible for. But in contemporary society, it is practically never so. Man becomes what is called an adult with such an imbalance in the development of his various parts that he must be "reharmonized" before any real work of education can begin. Such a work is only possible with a guide, in a school for work on oneself, where, whatever may be the order and the means, he comes to a view of his real situation, a knowledge of what he is and of what constitutes inner work for self-development. A man must be led to understand that he is dual—essence and personality. He has to see that his personality, sustained by his self-love, has wrongfully usurped the whole of his power and has completely expropriated all of his functions to serve its own ends. He must recognize that his essence, the authentic part of himself, has been left undeveloped: and he must undertake to re-establish a right balance in himself. This requires the weakening of personality to reduce it to its proper degree of strength, and the transcending of narrow personal self-love toward the development of a sense of oneself harmoniously connected to the whole of life. And this demands at the same time the development of essence, both as a result of shocks which awaken it and by the sort of work which is possible only under the direction of a higher consciousness, a work of enlarging the understanding at the cost of experiences consciously lived. In ordinary life, the center of gravity is in personality while essence sleeps. In a moment of consciousness, this inner polarity is reversed; personality stands aside, the center of gravity is in the essence which awakens and finds that to express itself in life it has at its disposal an apparatus complete to the extent that personality has loosened its grip. In a moment of consciousness, however brief, harmony is re-established between essence and the functions, between centers and their contents, and between real individuality and its manifestation in life.

Awakening to oneself and obstacles to awakening

THUS, the everyday life of man goes by with his real I asleep, and the first obstacle to the awakening of this real I, which is the beginning of his possible evolution, is that he does not see this sleep. Just as a sleeping man cannot appreciate the state of being awake, so there is nothing in the nature of man in a state of ordinary waking which can value the state of awakening of the real I—the state of presence to himself and self-consciousness.

A sleeping man can only carry on his daily life if he wakes up. For this purpose he has instinct enough—after sleep has completed its restorative function—to put it aside to fulfill his own need to live; and at the same time, life itself, which needs him, takes the trouble to draw him out of his sleep.

For the second awakening, everything is different. Man in the waking state may indeed sometimes have an intuition of what it might be, but this foretaste is rarely strong enough for him to feel the wish to be "truly" himself; and even more rarely is this "wish to be" acute enough for him to awaken, even for one instant, at this second level. Moreover, for daily life (his own life and the life around which calls him to participate) man has no need for this second awakening, and there is nothing provided in everyday life to arouse it. This second awakening is not necessary for him either organically or, so to say, quantitatively, and all the activities of our daily life can go on without it. Man has no need of it except qualitatively, for himself, and only special influences, outside himself, can make him realize this. Actually, this second awakening (traditional texts call it the "second birth") has to do only with his own life, the life of his inner "being," and his participation in a different world from the everyday world. If in a man himself there is no "inner demand" for another quality of life nor a strong enough "wish to be" (and this lack may come from his essence, from the conditions at his birth or from the education he received) there is no chance whatever that he will be open to the influences that could help him escape from the sleep of his I, nor that he will ever undertake the necessary efforts. But if there are no special influences present, there is again no chance whatever that he will escape from his sleep.

Even for those who have kept this "wish to be," this "inner longing" (a great many have it, at least during the first part of their lives) and who meet these special influences (such people are far fewer), the obstacles to this second awakening, the true awakening, are so immense that the vast majority of them never attain it.

The primary fact, from which flow directly and indirectly all the other difficulties, is that for man, such as he ordinarily is, it is practically an impossibility for him to see his real state. Even if to a certain degree he has this "wish for being" and this "inner longing" for a life of another quality than his daily life, he has very few means for recognizing the special moments, the shocks where, in a flash of truth, he has access to a state of more presence. And also, among the many surrounding influences which attract him, he has very little with which to distinguish those which really respond to this inner longing. To recognize what could help him in this direction calls for a special inner attitude of sincerity, free of conventions and acquired rules, which will allow him to see with complete "objectivity," and with an awareness of his own, both what he is and what the world around him is. A sincere view of things as they are is in fact his best chance. But man is not able to have this. All the ideas that he has built up, all his education, all his conditioning resist it. Furthermore, carried away by life and the incessant demands which it obliges him to respond to, he refuses to see that he is mechanical and asleep; he has no time to make room for his inner demand or his wish to be. Of the "objective conscience" that is the right of every human being, that is, his own inner consciousness, the being-consciousness that could offer him a direction in keeping with himself, what is accessible is buried under all the alien notions he has learned. And in the world around him, he can no longer tell what could really help him.

One major obstacle shuts a man into this situation—a conviction, solidly rooted in him, that such as he is he actually possesses an authentic individuality with the fundamental qualities that go with it—such as permanent presence and freedom or freedom of choice—and the faculties which come from it: a conscious state, the capacity of attention and the ability to will and to do.

Man, by and large, is satisfied to be as he is. He thinks that his shortcomings and his eventual unhappiness come solely from outer defects, and in his opinion changes are merely a matter of adjusting the balance, getting rid of some faults or strengthening certain qualities.

Even if someone tells him that he does not possess anything of all this, why should he believe it? And in these circumstances, why should he undertake the difficult work on himself which someone tells him is necessary to attain a state which he is already sure he possesses? What reason to believe the books or the voices which tell him he is a nonentity? And why put his situation to the test, at the risk of compromising it, as long as things are going as well as they are?

A man must have an exceptionally active inner consciousness, an implacable inner demand, and a wish to be himself which nothing can suppress, or he must have been beaten and disappointed by life to the point that its value and meaning have come into question; otherwise he has no reason to undertake a study of this kind.

Owing to the inveterate belief in a fictitious personality and the abnormal conditions which it sets up, man comes to live more and more in forgetfulness of his being and of his real self. Moreover, signs and indications that he is unable to remember himself, unable to remember what is most worthwhile in himself, show up in thousands of ways, but man neither "sees" them nor "hears" them. However, his life is spotted with significant incidents and with contradictions—he does not remember what he decides; he does not remember the promises made to himself or often those he makes to others; he does not remember what he said or felt a few hours or a few days ago; he starts to work at something and soon it bores him, and he no longer knows why he undertook the task. His interest constantly shifts and changes; he forgets how he thought, what he said. And these phenomena occur particularly often in everything that concerns himself and that specially affects all his attempts to work on himself. This "self-forgetting," this powerlessness to remember what is truly himself, is indeed his most characteristic trait and probably the true cause of all his behavior. Not having any fixed basis in himself, his theories, his opinions and his behavior are constantly changing, and are totally devoid of precision and stability. He has only an artificial stability supported by associations educated into him, settled habits and conditioning stemming from mental concepts, such as "honor," "honesty," "duty," and "law," artificially created by the surrounding culture. These have no relation, except accidentally, with what would be his real honesty and his true honor, if he were conscious of himself.

This continuous self-forgetting and the resulting absence of any authentic fixed point within himself accounts for the general behavior of man in front of himself and his circle of friends. It explains the way he is taken, whether he knows it or not, by everything around him, that is, his constant "identification" with what attracts him, and the continuous imagination he engages in at every turn. Thus, self-forgetfulness brings with it identification and imagination, and these are two other characteristic traits of man as he is now.

As for identification, man forgets himself and loses himself in all the problems, large or small, that he finds along the way. His interest, his attention are taken in turn by each problem and he completely forgets, behind this, the real goals which he had set himself. As soon as something occurs and grabs his interest, he "identifies" himself with this thing, for a moment devotes himself totally to it—even if it is only for a split second—until something else takes place which captures his attention and changes his interest. He occupies himself with this other thing, and the first one is put to sleep or falls into oblivion. In the end, man is constantly in a state of identification with one thing or another—what change are the successive objects of this identification. The degree of identification, that is, its mobility, or on the contrary its intensity of fixation, depends directly on the kind of attention—one might say the degree of interest—which the events arouse. Sometimes the attention is scattered and shifting, and the objects of identification constantly change (this is usually called "being spontaneous"); at other times the attention is held captive, fixed, concentrating all the man's interest and force till he sees only that particular point, loses sight of all the rest, and becomes insensitive to it (this is usually called "concentration"). In any case the result is the same—man is entirely taken by exterior events, he loses sight of the whole and in that whole what he loses sight of more particularly is himself. His attention is an attention in one direction, entirely turned toward the outside. But in order not to forget himself in the act of living, he would need to have an attention in two directions, turned both toward himself and toward the outside, an attention of a different kind which he knows nothing about, which he has not developed, and which he is usually incapable of. As soon as he begins to discover it, this different attention is immediately and totally recaptured by external attractions, and he falls back into identification.

Thus identification is everywhere and always in us, in the most subtle and pernicious forms. And the difficulty in freeing oneself from it is all the greater because in ordinary life identification is looked upon as an excellent quality. Spontaneity, zeal, enthusiasm, idealism, inspiration, concentration, even passion are socially acknowledged values and it is held to be impossible to do good work in any field without such "qualities." In fact, in such conditions, a man can often do good automatic work "with considerable profit," but he can do nothing which is really corresponding to himself and "his" life. He is perhaps a good social robot, but he is not a man nor is he a human "individuality."

For the man who has undertaken to be himself, identification is in fact one of the most terrible enemies. At the very moment he believes he is struggling against it, he is still in its clutches. The more he is interested in things, and particularly in work on himself, the more he gives them his time, his interest, his attention, the greater is the risk of identifying with them; thus a man who wishes to free himself from them must be constantly on guard. He who wishes to work to be himself must first remember himself and stop identifying. So long as a man identifies or is susceptible to identification, he is the slave of everything around him and almost anything can happen to him.

The most powerful, the most immediate identification, and

also the least visible, is a man's identification with the image he has formed of himself, of his personages, and his different I's. In fact, in a man as cut off from himself as he ordinarily is, a whole imaginary edifice constructed in the course of his "formation" replaces self-consciousness and acts for it. This imaginatively constructed self forms, together with identification and self-forgetfulness, the tripod of aberrations among which man lives and the tripod of major obstacles met with by anyone who wishes to free himself.

Before effective action can lead a man toward awakening, it is necessary to know the nature of the forces that keep him in sleep.

First of all, it must be understood that the sleep in which man lives is not ordinary sleep, but a hypnotic sleep. Man is as if hypnotized, and throughout his life this hypnotic state is continually maintained and strengthened. Everything happens as if there were a combination of "forces" for whose sake it would be useful and profitable to keep man in a hypnotic state in order to prevent him from seeing the truth and understanding his position. These are the forces of "life on earth" which require that man "feed" the earth, make it live, and that he not separate from it, which he might be inclined to do if he became aware of what in reality he is.

"There is an eastern tale," Gurdjieff says,[1] "which speaks about a very rich magician who had a great many sheep. But at the same time this magician was very mean. He did not want to hire shepherds, nor did he want to erect a fence about the pasture where his sheep were grazing. The sheep consequently often wandered into the forest, fell into ravines, and so on, and above all they ran away, for they knew that the magician wanted their flesh and skins and this they did not like.

1. Ouspensky, *In Search of the Miraculous*, p. 219.

"At last the magician found a remedy. He hypnotized his sheep and suggested to them first of all that they were immortal and that no harm was being done to them when they were skinned, that, on the contrary, it would be very good for them and even pleasant; secondly he suggested that the magician was a good master who loved his flock so much that he was ready to do anything in the world for them; and in the third place he suggested to them that if anything at all were going to happen to them it was not going to happen just then, at any rate not that day, and therefore they had no need to think about it. Further the magician suggested to his sheep that they were not sheep at all; to some of them he suggested that they were lions, to others that they were eagles, to others that they were men, and to others that they were magicians.

"And after this all his cares and worries about the sheep came to an end. They never ran away again but quietly awaited the time when the magician would require their flesh and skins."

This tale is a very good illustration of man's position. The vital force which animates him throughout life, rather than feeding the capacity for understanding through right seeing, feeds instead a capacity for imagination resulting from a hypnotic seeing which falsifies the appearance of things. Instead of a vision of reality in which he is part of a whole, in a place that is his own, man sees himself as an autonomous being ruling over this totality according to the flow of his own fantasy, and his fantasy usurps the place of his true consciousness.

The power of imagination and fantasy has perhaps been indispensable in the past and is still partly necessary for mankind because of the need of "Nature" for man's "work" (that is, his capacity to transform energy) in its present form. Undoubtedly this power has some connection with sex energy and the "magnetism" it releases; in any case it has the effect of maintaining man's life just as it is. Each time that dreams take the place of reality, each time a man takes himself to be a lion, an eagle or a magician, it is the power of imagination that is at work. It is called Kundalini in certain teachings. The original meaning of Kundalini is the primordial cosmic vital force, perhaps equivalent to the "libido" of some psychoanalytic schools. This original meaning is often lost, and in many schools, instead of designating the power of consciousness, Kundalini, even if presented otherwise, is actually nothing more than the power of imagination. This dreadful force can act in all of the centers—each has its own form of it, and with its help all the centers can be satisfied with the imaginary rather than with the real. Under its sway, men lose the sense of what they are, and soon—just as with "drugs"—they can no longer free themselves from it—they believe it is useful, even necessary, for their development while in fact it is a hindrance. If men could really see their true position and become aware of what it is, this view would be completely unbearable for them. They would seek a way out and they would find it, because one exists. But the force and the attraction of imagination, which keeps them in this state of hypnosis, prevents them from seeing what Gurdjieff calls the "terror of their situation." It prevents them at the same time from seeing the way out and prevents their escaping *en masse*, which would risk upsetting the balances of life.

Thus to awaken, for a man, means first of all to be dehypnotized—to escape from the power of imagination and to see things—and himself—freshly as they really are. In that lies the principal difficulty; but there is also the certainty that such an awakening is possible, because this hypnotic state comes from a deviation that is artificial and superimposed. Hypnotic sleep is not justified by organic laws, and without giving up the conditions necessary for the maintenance of organic planetary life, to which in one part of himself he belongs, a man can wake up.

Theoretically he can, but practically it is almost impossible because as soon as a man opens his eyes, and awakens for a moment, all the forces that keep him asleep begin to act on him again with tenfold energy, and he falls back immediately into sleep, very often dreaming that he is awake or awakening.

In ordinary sleep, a man who has difficulty in waking up—as sometimes happens—has definite tests of whether he is awake—he enters another state and can pinch himself to be sure that he has stopped sleeping. With hypnotic sleep it is different; there are no objective signs, at least when a man begins to awaken (later, however, signs do exist, but anyone who knew about them at the beginning would at once transform them into imagination and dreams). It is necessary that someone else, a man who is already awake, should arouse him out of his sleep so long as by himself he has not yet become able to wake up.

Returning to this imaginative power which prevents man from seeing things as they really are, observation shows that it arises at every moment, from every part of a man, and in a complex way. It permeates the life of man, especially of "modern" man. In order to try to understand it, we may suppose that it is actually manifested on two levels and produces at the same time two different films.

The first film is interpretive; it appears when a man is attentive to the external world and tries to adapt himself to its demands and its modifications. Starting from the necessarily relative perceptions he has of the world and from the relatively appropriate responses which he makes, he constructs an interpretive film which is more or less copied from the real world: it would be better to say more or less far removed from that real world.

The second film is imaginative, and it appears as soon as a

man is attentive to his inner psychic world. It is fashioned entirely from materials of this psychic world which are received and originally recorded from elements of reality, but in forms more or less distant from it. This second film thus has no direct correspondence with outer reality, thus no confrontation with reality can have spontaneous control over it; it may be completely cut off from reality, wandering wherever it pleases.

These two films, the interpretive and the imaginative, are being superimposed on real perceptions all the time by man's psychic activity. Both films are ceaselessly being fabricated by the mixing of these present perceptions with old material, and both are recorded simultaneously on the various rolls. In fact, without our knowing it, simple perception, interpretation and imagination are always present in us simultaneously. We live with the three kinds of seeing close together and nothing takes place in one of the three which does not cause a reverberation in the two others.

But what is most important is the sense and purpose of these films. If man were a completed being, knowing himself as he is, able to see reality directly and respond to it fully and harmoniously so far as he himself is concerned, his life would flow without shocks with the satisfaction of a task that has been fully assumed. He would have a constant vision of things as they are, a constant sense of the relativity of everything; and so these films would serve no purpose. But because man is an incompletely developed being, incapable of facing the realities of life and responding to them only in a partial or confused way, he would live in discord, anxiety and remorse for not being what he ought to be if his imaginative power did not ceaselessly wedge in this double film. Thanks to these films, man justifies himself for being what he is, stops noticing all his shortcomings, or, at least, finds them "normal" and stops suffering in relation to them.

At the same time, once a man has entered into this play of the imagination he no longer has any chance of escaping from it by himself. His attention is by nature weak—it does not generally enable him to hold more than one thing at a time in his field of vision—it is sometimes attracted toward perceptions of reality, sometimes toward the flow of interpretations, sometimes toward the constructs of imagination. It shifts continually from one to another, with the result that in man there is either one or another, usually without his having observed the switch. He never knows clearly which of the three fields he is in—and thus finally he loses any chance he had of being able to see and understand his situation.

In man such as he ordinarily is, the confusion between the three domains of perception—real, interpretive and imaginative—is so complete that he no longer has any sense of how they are related. In particular, he constantly confuses, substitutes, or identifies the real with the interpretive and makes use of one or the other indiscriminately according to which seems to him most opportune. On the other hand, he nearly always separates the imaginative kind of perception from, or even opposes it to, the two other kinds without realizing that it is made up (just as are dreams) of elements provided by them to a more or less distant, more or less unconscious degree. This imaginative domain is even one of the ways through which the recorded and often forgotten content of the other two domains can be brought to light.

Moreover, "by essence," the inner structure of different men is not the same in every case and their tendency to favor the real perception itself or to favor the run of one or the other of the films—either starting from the real perception or later quite independently of it—is not the same. This touches on the whole psychosomatic makeup and on the special relationship in each man between his two aspects. By nature he may be always favoring one or the other; he may respond to every impression, wherever it comes from, to every demand or incursion of outer or inner life in one way or the other. But since both have been fabricated out of real perception, there can be nothing in these films that is absolutely independent. This also bears on man's four fundamental ways of manifesting (one might say the four modes of automatic functioning of the machine) which are closely related to his fundamental type and the preponderance in him of the organic, emotional or the intellectual level or of a state of equilibrium which unites and perhaps transcends them. According to whether a man is led to prefer real perceptions, the interpretive, or the imaginative film, his life becomes balanced in different ways. And if he favors one or the other to an extreme he enters into the "world" of positivism, of neurosis or of psychosis. The last tendency, carried to its limit—the imaginative film fixed on a more or less narrow subject and cut off from any contact with reality—becomes obsession, delirium or madness. In any case, in one or the other of these three modes, and to the degree that it becomes exclusive, man is the victim of his imagination. The only mode in which imagination is not all-powerful, and is relatively held in check, is the fourth mode, the balanced mode. It constitutes the best basis for "work on oneself"; but it is rare, and the conditions of contemporary education seldom permit its formation.

By nature, and by the very fact of his existence, man cannot avoid having real perceptions, interpretations, and "imaginary" constructs; perhaps the possibilities inherent in such a combination are even one of the most profound reasons for man's existence. But as a result of his abnormal education and the abnormal conditions of his life, the way in which these three different elements are formed in him is totally distorted and out of balance. They rest almost entirely on "subjective" data and have lost all real objectivity. The emphasis given to the interpretive or imaginative films by almost all education and the whole of modern society, along with the preferred mode of reaction that each man is accustomed to give to his psychic or his somatic aspect, dominates his habitual manifestations and forms part of the natural, automatic functioning of almost all human machines. All these modes of functioning are, however, useless and generally harmful. They are nothing but an artificial covering developed under pressure of the imagination.

The only useful thing for man is the exact perception of impressions and the true "vision" of things as they are. The normal affirmation of self, resulting from these two faculties, could not possibly be the fancied reaction, more or less removed from reality, of an imagined and changing I. It would be the true "response" brought forth by an authentic presence, conforming exactly to the real facts and the laws that govern their evolution. Nor does this "response" require "imagination," that fallacious imagining in which men usually lose themselves, but an objective representation resulting from exact interpretation of what is seen and a previsioning of it in conformity with real knowledge.

Everywhere in the world today praises are sung for the richness and merits of the realm of imagination or of "creative imagination." This faculty is considered one of the great assets of our time. On the one hand, these claims stem from the fact that in imagination man gives himself—and men give one another—the satisfactions that they have need of, whereas life—that is, abnormal life—hardly gives them any. It is easier to imagine one's life than to transform it. On the other hand, these claims come from an intuition that a man worthy of the name, endowed with knowledge, should in fact foresee and organize his life; so, without the means to do this, ordinary man immediately attributes both this and many other qualities to himself in an imaginary form.

Actually, imagination in all its forms is one of man's worst enemies and one of the main obstacles to his awakening and his evolution. A man can undertake nothing so long as he does not begin to see things simply as they are. Then he can acquire an understanding and only later does an authentic "imagination" become possible for him, that is to say, that law-conformable "previsioning" which is indeed one of the major faculties of a man worthy of the name.

These three fundamental facts—man's forgetfulness of his real I, his automatic fabrication in its stead of imaginative constructs, and man's constant identification of himself with everything that happens to him—explain in large part his ordinary way of living.

In place of the real I which is absent (it is asleep), a surface personality develops with many facets more or less connected with one another, but often contradictory to each other or turned in different directions. These are the different little I's, each one of which enables a man, according to rules that have been learned, to face one of the typical situations of his life and in each of which he firmly believes when it appears.

This assemblage, artificially built up by the play of life, by education, imitation, by the acquisition of habits and of "buffers" (of which we shall have more to say), ascribes to itself many qualities of which only a semblance exists and which have no correspondence to reality: unity, continuity and various powers such as knowing, foreseeing, choosing, deciding, organizing and doing. Actually, for man as he is, all these powers are illusory.

What gives man the illusion of his unity or his integrity is partly the sensation he has of his physical body which always appears to stay the same, and partly his name, by which he is "known" and which in general does not change in spite of the succession of different personages.

Moreover, there are a certain number of mechanisms and habits implanted in him by education or acquired by imitation and, last but not least, the system of buffers which neutralize in him all sense of self-contradiction. Always experiencing the same physical sensations, hearing himself called by the same name, finding the same habits and inclinations in himself that he has always known, not feeling his inner contradictions and never putting anything in question, man imagines that he is always the same.

In reality, aside from external appearance, there is nothing permanent in him, everything changes without ceasing: there is no single controlling center nor a permanent I, and the personage which represents man in life is nothing but an artificial construction.

But that is not all. The totality of personal interpretations and illusions making up the various personages with which a man appears in life is jealously defended, in his outer as well as his inner manifestations, by the feeling of self-righteousness necessary to the image he has built up, and the least affront is felt as a setback or loss. This feeling, which artificially welds the whole edifice together, is self-love.

Man is weak. He is as weak as a child and in his own being, in his essence, he is really nothing but a child. In moments of sincerity he knows this, and events in his life make him feel responsible for feeling it. But instead of recognizing this and undertaking the necessary efforts (but he does not know which efforts, and he is lazy) and asking for the help that he needs (but he does not know where or how to ask, and he has lost the necessary simplicity), a man prefers to defend before and against everything this picture he has of himself and his "ideal" of "what he ought to be." Every time this image, which he believes in, is threatened, he feels as if he were personally threatened. He reacts immediately in its defense, in exactly the same way as a child defends a doll. This senseless attachment to an image, which is largely fallacious and on behalf of which all his reactions arise, is the very foundation of his self-love and one of the greatest obstacles to his seeing what he really is, as well as being an obstacle to the awakening of his higher I (that is, to the growth of his essence).

Self-love and defending this image of himself are basic in man's usual relations with his fellow man. These are generally governed by what one could call "inner considering," a condition in which a man is mostly preoccupied with what people think of him and what he should do to be recognized and appreciated in accordance with the image of himself he wants to give. As this image is generally "idealized" and somewhat exaggerated, he always considers that he is not appreciated enough, that he is not given his proper place, that people are not polite enough to him, that he is not appreciated at his true worth. How people look at him, what they think of him, takes on an enormous importance in his eyes. All this worries and preoccupies him; he wastes his time and energy on conjectures and speculations. If he feels a little bit misunderstood he becomes suspicious, distrustful, even hostile toward others and in this way he develops a negative attitude which only aggravates his situation. But things can go still further—a man can feel himself thwarted by his surroundings, by the society he lives in, the events that take place, even the weather. Everything he dislikes appears to him as an affront and seems unjust, illegitimate, or wrong. Everybody is wrong, even the weather is at fault—only he is right.

This is not to say that there is nothing for a man to defend in life. But what he really ought to defend (the manifestation of his own nature and of his own being in a form which belongs uniquely to him and under the control of real self-love) appears only with the awakening and development of his higher I and has nothing to do with his many I's or his self-image.

"'Buffer' is a term which requires special explanation. We know what buffers on railway carriages are. They are the contrivances which lessen the shock when the carriages strike one another. If there were no buffers the shock of one carriage against another would be very unpleasant and dangerous. Buffers soften the results of these shocks and render them unnoticeable and imperceptible.

"Exactly the same appliances are to be found within man. They are created, not by nature but by man himself, although involuntarily. The cause of their appearance is the existence in man of many contradictions; contradictions of opinions, feelings, sympathies, words, and actions. If a man throughout the whole of his life were to feel all the contradictions that are within him he could not live and act as calmly as he lives and acts now. He would have constant friction, constant unrest. We fail to see how contradictory and hostile the different I's of our personality are to one another. If a man were to feel all these contradictions he would feel what *he really is*. He would feel that he is mad. It is not pleasant for anyone to feel that he is mad. Moreover, a thought such as this deprives a man of self-confidence, weakens his energy, deprives him of 'self-respect.' Somehow or other he must master this thought or banish it. He must either destroy contradictions or cease to see and to feel them. A man cannot destroy contradictions. But if 'buffers' are created in him he can cease to feel them and he will not feel the impact from the clash of contradictory views, contradictory emotions, contradictory words.

"'Buffers' are created slowly and gradually. Very many 'buffers' are created artificially through 'education.' Others are created under the hypnotic influence of all surrounding life. A man is surrounded by people who live, speak, think, and feel by means of 'buffers.' Imitating them in their opinions, actions, and words, a man involuntarily creates similar 'buffers' in himself. 'Buffers' make a man's life more easy. It is very hard to live without 'buffers.' But they keep man from the possibility of inner development because 'buffers' are made to lessen shocks and it is only shocks that can lead a man out of the state in which he lives, that is, waken him. 'Buffers' lull a man to sleep, give him the agreeable and peaceful sensation that all will be well, that no contradictions exist and that he can sleep in peace. *'Buffers' are appliances by means of which a man can always be in the right.* 'Buffers' help a man not to feel his conscience,"[1] and tranquilize his self-love.

When a man becomes aware of his real situation in a sudden glimpse of truth or is affected by an unexpected shock which blocks his protective mechanisms, such as a sudden setback or serious danger, he has an opportunity for an instant to understand two things. The first thing is that he has none of the qualities which he prides himself on; and the second is that he is dual, that he has two natures and that behind the ordinary man sleeps a real I which contains the possibility of these qualities and which the shock has awakened for an instant. For an instant he sees that a surface personage, an artificial "personality," is in charge, and, endowed with illusory powers, is answering in his stead to everything in life. In these glimpses he can understand that he needs to become truly himself and that if he really "wishes" to become himself, henceforward only one thing is important—to wake up, to attain self-awakening, the awakening and growth of being. And he can see that this personality, this personage which he believes in so firmly, which takes up all the room and under whose influence he lives, is the chief obstacle to the awakening of the real I.

1. Ouspensky, *In Search of the Miraculous*, pp. 154-155.

Each moment when he sees that he is asleep, and that to become himself he must at all costs wake up, a man, if he is honest, experiences in himself the need to dislodge this personality which gets in his way and he begins to struggle against it. From then on, a new scale of values appears for him—all that helps his awakening is good for him, all that prevents it is evil. The only real "sin" for such a man comes to be whatever prevents his inner being from awakening.

But man has no power over these moments of self-consciousness. They appear and disappear under the influence of outer conditions, accidental associations, shocks, memories and emotions, none of which depend on him.

Yet in fact, by right methods and properly directed efforts, man could acquire control over these moments and become conscious of himself. It would be possible for him to achieve mastery over these fleeting moments of awareness, to evoke them more often, to keep them longer, and even to make them permanent. But he cannot do this by himself—a development of that order implies knowledge and the use of means which man as he is neither possesses nor knows how to put into practice. When he has given up the illusion of being equipped with qualities and powers which undoubtedly should belong to him but which he does not have, man must give up another illusion—that he can obtain anything in this realm by himself. As soon as he tries to wake up, man perceives that to wish for it is not enough—left to himself he goes back to sleep and does not wake up again.

As long as a man has not gone through this, has not suffered from it and has not experienced fully the difficulty of awakening, he is not able to understand that for this aim long and hard work is necessary which it is impossible to do by himself.

Speaking in general, what is necessary to awaken a sleeping man? A good shock is necessary. But when a man is fast asleep one shock is not enough. A long period of continual shocks is needed, and the shocks must come from outside. The man must be placed in conditions where someone else, or the conditions themselves, administer these shocks to him and the shocks must be repeated as long as it takes to awaken him.

To ask someone else for help is not much use; very soon, like everyone else, this one also falls asleep, is taken by something else, and fails to awaken him. A man really capable of staying awake is needed, but such a man has his own work, his own tasks to carry out, and in general has other things to do than waste his time waking others up—usually he has no reason to take on this task.

There is also the possibility of turning to outer conditions to be woken up by mechanical means. For this an alarm clock is necessary. But the trouble is that a man gets accustomed to the alarm clock far too quickly; he simply stops hearing it. Many alarm clocks, with different bells or buzzers, are therefore necessary. A man must literally surround himself with alarm clocks which will prevent him from sleeping. But here again there are difficulties. Alarm clocks must be wound up; to remember about this one must wake up often. But what is still worse—a man soon gets used to all sorts of alarm clocks and after a certain time he only sleeps the better for them. Therefore, the alarms must be constantly changed; new ones must continually be invented. In the course of time, this may help a man to awaken; but there is very little chance of a man doing all the work of inventing, winding up and changing all these clocks by himself, without outside help. It is much more likely that he will begin this work and before long will fall asleep and that in sleep he will dream that he is inventing alarm clocks, winding them up and changing them—and finally be sleeping all the sounder.

Therefore, in order to awaken, a combination of efforts is needed. It is essential that there should be somebody to wake the sleeping man up; it is essential that somebody should look after the man who wakes him; it is essential to have alarm clocks, and it is also essential continually to invent new ones. Finally, to get results in an enterprise like this, the only way is for a certain number of people to pool their efforts.

One man alone can do nothing.

One man alone can easily deceive himself and take for awakening what is simply a new dream. If a certain number of people have decided to work together against sleep, they will wake each other up, and even if most of them go to sleep again it may be enough for one to wake up and for him to wake the others. In the same way they will share their various methods of awakening. All together they can be a great help to each other, while without mutual help each of them alone would attain nothing.

A man who wants to awake must look for other people who also want to awake and work together with them.

But even this is not enough because such an undertaking requires knowledge which an ordinary man does not possess. The work must be organized and directed in accordance with this knowledge. Without these conditions the efforts made are more than likely to be useless or go astray. People can invent all kinds of methods and means, they may even undertake "asceticisms" and torture themselves; but all these efforts will be useless if they are not carried out in "a certain way," precisely that way which will lead to transformation. For many people, this is the most difficult thing to understand. It is not every effort that leads to awakening. Efforts of a special kind are needed and these vary according to the surrounding conditions and the time.

But there are even greater difficulties—for intellectuals especially. By themselves and on their own initiative, following what they think or believe best for themselves, people are capable of great efforts and great sacrifices. But they cannot understand that all these intended sacrifices corresponding to their personal ideas have probably nothing to do with what is needed for the awakening they are searching for, if only because they know nothing about this awakening. They cannot admit that in this case all their sacrifices are bound to be useless. And they cannot understand that their first effort, their first sacrifice, ought to be to renounce their personal ideas and beliefs in favor of obedience to another.

This kind of work must be organized. And it can be organized only by a man who knows its problems and its aims, its rules and its methods, and has in the course of his life had the experience of passing through such an organized work himself.

Those who are able to organize and assist in such work have their own tasks and aims. They know the value of their time; they know that time is counted and they put a very high price on it. This is another reason why a man on his own has little chance of receiving help. Not only is his isolation itself an unfavorable situation, but a man who takes charge of a work on awakening would prefer to help, say, twenty or thirty people who want to awake rather than one person. And so the man who wants to stay on his own runs the risk of cutting himself off.

For the man who wishes to awaken and has begun to study himself, his first aim must be to find a group. Self-study can be brought to a successful result only in a properly organized group.

But for a long time the work itself will be only a preparatory work. So many things in the human machine are broken or rusty that preliminary repairs are first necessary. Real work toward awakening can only be undertaken later on a solid and balanced foundation.

Except in extreme cases where separate personal work is necessary, the preparatory work also is only possible in a group. One man alone cannot see himself. But a number of people who come together for this purpose will help one another, even involuntarily. It is characteristic of human nature always to see the faults of others more easily than one's own—this happens very "spontaneously." But on the path of self-study a man soon learns that he has in himself all the characteristics and faults that he sees in others—the difference is only in degree. There are many things that he does not see in himself, whereas in other people he begins to see them. If he has really understood that these features, in varying degrees, are also in him, he can begin to pay attention to them, see them, rediscover them in himself and even actually experience them—the other members of the group act as a kind of mirror in which he can see himself. But in order to see himself in the features, defects and faults of his fellow-workers and not just see their features and faults, he needs to have a special inner attitude, a vigilance, an attention of a particular direction and quality, which requires great honesty and above all great sincerity toward himself. A man can only speak honestly about what he himself has experienced. Complete sincerity and willingness to put oneself in question again and again must be respected by each member of the group, or such a work is not possible; the failure of one person is enough to "defile the atmosphere."

Thus, in the work of self-study, each student begins to accumulate material resulting from his observations within himself. Here again group work is indispensable. Twenty people will have twenty times as much material, most of which can be used by everyone. The exchange of observations and later the sharing of their understanding is one of the purposes of the existence of work groups.

But above all, each student must remember that he is not one—that one part of him is the man who wants to awaken, but the other part, his personality, has no desire whatever to awaken and has to be brought to it in spite of itself by the use at the same time of force and cunning. A group is usually a pact concluded between the real I's of a number of people to engage in a common struggle against their false personalities. The real I of each of them is either powerless against his personality or is asleep; so personality is in control of the situation. But if twenty I's join together to struggle against each of their personalities they can become stronger than it; in any case they can disturb its dominance and prevent the other I's from sleeping so peacefully.

However, self-observation by itself is not sufficient for awakening. It is only a preliminary step requiring a certain degree of awakening, but the awakening remains in a certain sense passive—man has hardly emerged from sleep before he falls back into it.

It is only in beginning to "remember himself" that a man really begins to awaken: in trying to rediscover, collect, and live what, behind these personages, he feels to be more truly himself. This effort brings an "impression of oneself" with a special "taste" which cannot be mistaken—when a man experiences it, he begins to be less imposed upon by his personality. What this effort actually implies cannot be described in words: it is a personal experience which like all experience of consciousness only has meaning when it is lived through and at the moment it is lived through, and only for the man who lives through it.

As long as a man cannot remember himself, things happen in him or because of him but they are not done in his presence or by himself. Only the machine functions; he himself is not present—even simple self-observation is not possible without a certain degree of self-remembering. So long as man, through self-remembering, and the relative knowledge of himself he finds in it, does not come to a real "presence to himself" in a sufficiently global way, things are neither done by him nor with him.

It is only in beginning "to remember himself" that a man can truly awaken. It is only with a real and long enough awakening that a man becomes present to himself. And it is only with "presence to himself" that a man begins to live like a man.

The first step in self-study: inner quiet, relaxation, sensation of oneself, and the attempt to remember oneself

THE ideas presented in the preceding chapters may have shown us how superficial is the "knowledge" we have about ourselves and our lives. If we want really to live our life, perhaps we now feel the need to deepen our understanding of it.

This places us in front of a new demand, something we have never looked at in this way until now. The precise reasons why we want to undertake this study are doubtless a little different for everyone, and the specific aim which we have in view may not appear to be the same in each case and can be formulated in various ways. Nevertheless, each of these aspects is related to the same inner demand—to give our life a direction and meaning which in all honesty we have not yet found for it or, in any case, only found in part.

Almost everything we have done up until now has been directed outwardly—the outer world has absorbed almost all of our life. In comparison, the amount of time actually spent in turning toward ourselves and our inner life is insignificant. In our training, schooling and daily activities, almost everything has been focused on externals. We are oriented toward knowledge coming from outside; we have learned to look only outside ourselves, and to deal with people, things and external circumstances. Even our "prayers" turn out most often to be directed outwardly, to an external God. We have learned very little about turning toward ourselves—it happens only briefly and at long intervals. If, however, we want to attain our own aims in life, and if we wish for a life with achievements and qualities like those we feel called to attain, and with achievements which have the taste of the truths we have realized, certainly this cannot exist as long as outer life constantly carries us away. We need to develop in ourselves a strong, lucid, stable presence, one that is capable of achieving its goals, making use of the forces that can help us, and resisting the forces in life that carry us away. And, first of all, we need to be continuously and fully ourselves in front of and in the midst of life.

Most of us have made some efforts in this direction, but we already see that these are almost always scattered, uncoordinated, disconnected, and completely inadequate. At best, a certain self-control and "will" have been developed at the cost of struggle and inner division, which has led to surrender to the opposing forces, or a revulsion against them. Even this control is precarious and constantly in question. We cannot say that it has brought us to be fully ourselves or that we have realized synthesis and harmony within ourselves, or between ourselves and life—it is not what could be called the first step toward self-realization or even realization of the lucid and stable presence which we understood that we needed. If we wish to reach something of real value in this direction, we feel now that it is necessary to begin a work of another order, a work that is much better structured.

One thing is certainly true today. We cannot go further in our search for more presence in life conditions without first turning inwardly toward ourselves, without more experience and understanding of what we are, and without developing qualities we still lack. It is only in and through ourselves that what can give meaning to our lives is perceived and comes to pass.

But we have not learned how to turn to ourselves; we do not know at all what an inner work toward awakening and self-development could be. Just as we had to learn to manifest in our outer work, we must recognize that we are going to have to learn what inner work is and what kind of action or activity it requires.

Confronted with this first necessity to deepen our knowledge of ourselves, we suddenly see what an immense undertaking it is—just as large as, if not larger than, the training necessary for our outer life. It is also a long road, sometimes boring, and often even discouraging; and from the beginning difficulties appear. Where to begin? We see clearly that a much longer, more intense, and more exacting work is necessary than any attempts of this kind we have ever made before. It will require methods of which we are totally ignorant. If we want to succeed in this, a much more organized work is needed.

A suitable structure cannot come from us—we do not have sufficient knowledge. A man who knows is necessary. And we cannot accomplish such a work on our own: alone we would not have the amount of time, all the different capacities, nor even the necessary courage. The first absolutely essential condition is to find a group of seekers interested in this work to whom the knowledge which is indispensable has been given. To find such a group is in itself extremely unusual and difficult.

Let us suppose that by some miracle these conditions are realized and we can join a group which has undertaken to work along these lines. Even then, we shall never have the necessary interest to carry out this work if we do not have a clear enough vision of the direction to be followed, and if we do not understand the meaning of these first efforts.

We have seen that three different levels can be recognized in us, three very different modes of activity—an instinctive-moving level, an emotional level and an intellectual level. We are not without some experience in each of these domains, and we could begin our studies with any one of them.

Thus we could begin at the emotional level, that is to say, with all our emotions or feelings. But those of us who have tried (and others may very quickly come to the same conclusion) find out that our emotions and our feelings are probably just the place where we are most helpless. They rise up, disappear, make us blind, or carry us away in spite of ourselves, and they are certainly neither a solid nor a favorable foundation for beginning self-study.

We could also begin at the intellectual level. But we all know how much our thoughts are connected together, form associations, run on in spite of us, and escape us. We all know how difficult it is for us to "hold" them—to hold our attention on an intellectual task. And so this also does not seem an easy work with which to begin our self-study.

Lastly, there is the organic level—our body. It is solid and concrete, with an apparently stable form which can, in any case, be relied on to some degree. It is the instrument through which we perceive and our means of action. It can stay still voluntarily and thus is easier than the other parts for us to observe. It is relatively obedient, and we have a certain amount of control over it (in any case more than over our other parts). In addition, it is the one solid material base in us, and as a general rule everything undertaken on earth, whether human or not, must first be established on a solid and firm foundation. Finally, it is through the body that all the exchanges of life take place and through which we receive all the energies we need. For all these reasons, it may be wise to begin our work with it; and we need to be wise because we have a difficult task. If we don't go about it intelligently, with a certain artfulness, we can be sure that stupidity will lead us to bitter disappointments.

If we wish to study our body, or at least, to begin with, its moving function, its movement, we must first of all be related to it. What relates us to the body is the sensation we have of it—the inner perception of my physical being, the physical sensation of myself. But sensation has an even greater importance because, if our aim is eventually to develop a stable presence in ourselves, the sensation of our physical being is an inherent part of this. It is the most concrete and easily controlled part.

We always have some sensation of our body; otherwise our postures could not be maintained, our movements would be made haphazardly, or not at all. But we are not conscious of this sensation, we are unaware of it, except in extreme situations when an unusual effort is required or when something suddenly goes badly or goes wrong. The rest of the time we forget about it. In order to know and observe ourselves and to study our body and later to support our work, we need to have this sensation. This calls for a new relationship to come into existence in me: I—conscious of—my sensation. Actually much more than just a new connection is involved. Really a new situation arises within us in this effort and, undoubtedly, this is what is most important, but we do not yet have enough actual experience to speak of it.

What we need immediately is a stable sensation; that is, we need to develop a more steady and longer lasting consciousness of our body and its situation. The first idea which then comes to mind, of course, is to try to follow this awareness of our body in the midst of the movements and activities of our life. We can try; but we soon see, on the one hand, that the sensation never remains the same so that it is extremely difficult to stay in touch with it and, on the other hand, that our activities distract us and cause us to lose all possibility of following our situation.

In fact, if we wish to experience sensation of ourselves and to develop the possibility of remaining aware of it, we must work in much less difficult conditions. We must put ourselves in specially favorable circumstances which correspond to what is possible for us; and, at the start, in a field we do not know yet, where nothing is developed as it should be, almost nothing is possible for us.

Moreover, in our work on ourselves, it will always be so. This work only makes sense if it enables us one day to go into life in order to manifest there to the full that which we recognize as being and to accomplish what depends on us. There will always be two lines in our work on ourselves: on the one hand, inner work in quiet conditions suitable for the development of certain possibilities, and on the other, putting ourselves to the test in life, to an extent proportionate to the inner development that has been realized. But life is a tempest in which one must be very strong inwardly not to be upset by the opposing elements. And before putting ourselves to the test or taking big risks, it is necessary to have developed patiently, in sheltered and favorable conditions, the forces and faculties (powers) which will preserve us from disaster.

As regards the sensation of ourselves, before being able to follow how it changes as we move about and live, we need to know it in a basic condition where we can immediately return to it, always the same, whenever it is needed for our inner work. Just as a zero or a norm is needed in all measurement, in the same way we need a point of reference in evaluating ourselves, a yardstick, the measure of a situation that is always the same. And for the sensation of oneself, we can find this base only in complete relaxation.

We must therefore put ourselves in conditions where complete relaxation is possible. Having realized this is necessary, we must promise ourselves to try it every day, so far as this is honestly possible, at least once, if not twice, and perhaps even more.

We shall put ourselves in conditions where we are sure we will not be disturbed, nor have to respond to any calls from outer life. And, first of all, we have to take a posture suitable to work of this kind. Any such posture must be stable in itself, comfortable, and without strain of any kind. For us, the one which is probably the best is simply sitting in a straight-backed chair or in an armchair if necessary, with the lower back supported or not, but with the pelvis well-balanced, the body erect and the head straight, that is, neither too low (which is a sign of inertia and even sleep) nor too high (a sign of running away into the intellect and ideas and even imagination). The eyes may be left open or closed. If the eyes are open, what is seen can feed the association of ideas in ourselves which takes up our attention and turns us away from our search—thus in this case it is desirable to keep looking steadily at a fixed point one or two yards in front of one. If the eyes are closed, not seeing anything external brings about greater quiet but also favors inertia and giving in to sleep. The knees should be at right angles and the feet close together or only slightly apart, flat on the ground. The arms and shoulders should hang freely, with the forearms bent, each hand flat on the corresponding knee; in this position, the energy circuit passing through the hands is left open. The hands may also be placed in front of one, the right hand palm upwards in the left; then the energy circuit is closed in its natural direction (reverse the hands for left-handers).

It is a fact that there are various circuits of energy in our organism. Some of these are well known, such as the circuit of blood circulation or of the nerve impulses. Others, such as the circuits of the autonomic nervous system, are much less known or practically unknown to us, as is the case with the circuits of more subtle energies. At the very most we have heard they may exist. One of the reasons for taking the posture which we have adopted for all intensive inner work is to allow a free flow everywhere within us for all these circuits of energy. Another reason is that it makes total quiet possible; that is, on the one hand it does not cause mechanical discomfort in any part of the body or any uncomfortable pressure on our organs; and on the other hand it allows all unnecessary tensions to be dissolved, starting with those of our physical body. In a human being everything is connected. Mechanical pressures and especially muscular tensions block the free circulation of our energies, and they have their counterpart in the other parts of ourselves where there are similar features which prevent or divert work on ourselves. If for some reason (for example, a deformation of the skeleton) these cannot be resolved, we need to be aware of them in order to bring about as far as possible the necessary adjustments at the different levels within us.

A favorable posture for intensive work on oneself must therefore be perfectly balanced and naturally stable, the vertebral column and the head held upright on a perfectly stable pelvis without any kind of tension other than the very light tension at the back of the neck which prevents the head falling forward. This is the least tension necessary as a support for the effort of watchfulness.

The posture considered the best since ancient times, especially in the East where men practice these exercises a great deal, is the "lotus position." With the buttocks slightly raised (on a cushion) to an extent which varies for each person, this posture provides the most stable base of any, the broadest area of contact with the ground and the most balanced immobility of the vertebral column. But for Westerners, due to their lack of practice since childhood and their somewhat different skeletal formation, it is generally impossible. Nevertheless we can take a half-lotus position, or simply the posture of sitting on the ground with legs crossed. Even these intermediate positions are often difficult at first and require a certain amount of "training." They are not absolutely necessary, and in the beginning the simple sitting position that we first described is perfectly suitable for work on oneself. But the other positions are the best for intensive inner work. They allow the greatest freedom with the least tension, the least expenditure of energy for the organism as a whole. Moreover each one of us has particular differences which require that everyone should find the position which is the most balanced for himself or herself.

A position which might seem the most natural of all for resolving all tensions is lying flat on one's back. But this position, besides eliminating all muscular tension and leading first to inner passivity and then to sleep, also favors the circulation and development of instinctive forces so that the general equilibrium is upset and made less sensitive, which is not desirable. Nevertheless, in some special cases or at special times, it may be the only position which gives enough relaxation. Provided that we can recognize and actually correct the disequilibrium, this position also permits intensive work on oneself.

So, having placed ourselves in conditions where we are sure we will not be disturbed externally, we shall choose this seated position which at the beginning is certainly adequate for the work we intend to do and is the simplest one for us. First, we have to re-establish quiet conditions inside ourselves and free ourselves little by little from all the outer preoccupations of daily life, the tensions they create, the hold and the inner repercussions they have on us, and the agitation they cause. This requires more or less time depending upon each person's state, how well he knows how to work and the pressure exerted by the outer circumstances.

Next, there is a necessary initial step, whatever work exercise is being practiced: this is always to remind ourselves why we are undertaking this effort and to find again in ourselves that which feels a need for this work and the line of interest it is connected to. An exercise of this kind has no meaning unless it is connected each time to our need to become a little more ourselves.

When we feel this we see that we are always divided—one part of us needs this effort and willingly accepts to make it; another part which may be more or less powerful (this can change with the weather or the circumstances) has no need for it at all and wants to have nothing to do with it. This other part has no interest in it whatever and would prefer something quite different—such as listening to music, going to the theater or to the cinema, studying, dancing, etc.

We must convince this other part for one moment to help us, or at least not to interfere with us, even if it has to be given what satisfaction it needs later. And it is most important to get this agreement in order to reduce the conflicts within us to a minimum. Work of this kind requires a harmonious "atmosphere." It is better never to force anything.

Sometimes, however, at the risk of making no more efforts and seeing the part of us which has the most right to life wither away, we must compel the other part which smothers the first and refuses to make room for it to allow us to attempt what we wish. We must know how to do this when it appears to be necessary and demand of ourselves a discipline without useless struggle. We must be clever yet firm, knowing that each time we force something a resistance of equal strength is created. Even if the resistance created by constraint does not arise right away, it remains in the background, grows and gets larger through repeated accumulation until finally it explodes with destructive effects. It is necessary to know it, to observe it in oneself and to act accordingly. If this resistance is provoked or if it finds allies in oneself, it can make all real work impossible for a time. One must know how to recognize it, because there is nothing worse than undertaking an exercise of this kind without any real motive, simply because it has been suggested and we wish to get it over with. It is certainly more intelligent to wait for a better moment; at the same time, to put off until later what we cannot do right away is an obvious trap, a mild form of surrender to make the work more acceptable to the one who does not wish it. But to wait for a definite interval until a time precisely fixed in advance and then, at that moment, whatever the conditions may be, to begin relentlessly to make the effort again, is sometimes a justifiable expedient—though not without risks. Is this not what we do in our daily life for much less important goals?

Only if we are determined to bring about these first conditions, and only if we succeed in doing so, can we consider what should be our first efforts of work on ourselves. For these attempts bring nothing of themselves. They are only preparation for a long series of inner work efforts, difficult, sometimes exacting, strewn with pitfalls and dead ends where the risk of going astray is as great as it is in outer life, and the amount of work to be done is much greater and more subtle than in any other kind of endeavor. Initially, this work will most often be a matter of relaxation and sensation, later of self-remembering, following precise methods and under the surveillance of what it brings with it. To lose our way at this beginning may compromise any chance of future development, and from this point on we must abandon all abstract conceptions. Only the direct relationship of man to man, older to younger, master to disciple, will advance our progress from now on. A very alive inner awareness and a determination that never loses courage are indispensable to proceed on a road that is my own.

However, everything is relative, since human beings do not all possess the same possibilities for evolution; but all of us have a way we can (and should) follow, and which for us is essential. This way goes through precise stages, but at the same time the order in which they are reached and the means used to pass through them vary with each way and each school. Nor is the final level of attainment the same on the different ways. But in spite of these different aspects, what is possible to man in general, and the methods of his eventual evolution, obey the same laws and the same rules everywhere.

All of this is connected with the reasons why the exercises for work on oneself given in schools are not committed to writing. Or, if they are, such writings are accessible only to people who already have enough experience of the exercises and have practiced them long enough under the direction of their elders to understand what they stand for within the line of work of the particular school.

All the same, there is no secrecy involved. There is only the fact that nobody can understand experiences of this kind without having undergone them himself. A false understanding, be it insufficient, partial or mistaken, is the worst thing that can happen to the individual as well as to the school—thus everything possible is done to avoid it.

Conscience calls me to be myself.

To be myself begins with self-knowledge.

Self-knowledge begins with work on myself.

Work on myself is based on the sensation of myself.

THE situation of a man who has woken up to the need to be himself is difficult at all levels and necessitates three permanent lines of related effort:

Re-cognition.[1]
Conscious work.
Voluntary suffering.[2]

The precise form of these efforts takes on a different aspect at each level of development. The first of these aspects, at the level of awakening to oneself, consists of:

Submission to a higher level of consciousness.

Work toward being oneself through self-remembering and efforts of self-awareness.

Accepting to sacrifice one's ordinary life to the extent necessary for freeing oneself from it and trying to have it serve the work on oneself.

1. Recognition in the full sense of the word (not only in the sense of gratitude).

2. Suffering voluntarily accepted (which could also be called sacrifice) as an unavoidable element of efforts for inner transformation through the struggle of yes and no—not suffering unnecessarily sought after for a so-called "ascetic" aim—such ascetic practices and voluntary "mortifications" reverse the forces in play and are (except at certain precise moments) almost always useless, if not harmful.

THE situation [illegible]

[illegible]

1. Recognition in the full sense of the word (not only in [illegible] gratitude).
2. Suffering voluntarily accepted [illegible]